Africa and the Challenge of Development

Africa and the Challenge of Development

Acquiescence and Dependency versus Freedom and Development

AHMAD ABUBAKAR

PRAEGER

New York
Westport, Connecticut
London

Library of Congress Cataloging-in-Publication Data

Abubakar, Ahmad.
  Africa and the challenge of development.

  Bibliography: p.
  1. Africa—Economic policy. 2. Africa—Economic
conditions—1960- . 3. Africa—Dependency on
foreign countries. 4. Economic assistance—Africa.
I. Title.
HC800.A53   1989   338.96   88-32290
ISBN 0-275-93221-4 (lib. bdg. ; alk. paper)

Copyright © 1989 by Ahmad Abubakar

Library of Congress Catalog Card Number: 88-32290
ISBN: 0-275-93221-4

First published in 1989

Praeger Publishers, One Madison Avenue, New York, NY   10010
A division of Greenwood Press, Inc.

Printed in the United States of America

The paper used in this book complies with the Permanent Paper Standard issued by
the National Information Standards Organization (Z39.48–1984).

10 9 8 7 6 5 4 3 2 1

Contents

Preface

This book, spanning three years of effort, derives from some years of experience in dealing with development issues. Therefore it is not a theoretical work; it is practically oriented.

A lot has been said and written about African development since independence, much of it from theorists of economic development as well as from UN agencies, but little from practitioners in government directly involved with development work. Consequently the thrust has been to explain underdevelopment in terms of the conventional wisdom: lack of capital, manpower, colonial history, and so on. In this work I argue that Africa's development problems should be seen instead in terms of dependency and lack of commitment to develop. I am aware of the African center-periphery and Latin American-dependency theories. These have gone a long way in explaining underdevelopment, but one factor that has not received adequate attention is the attitude of African governments. The usual thinking blames underdevelopment on colonialism and also makes aid a vital resource for development. Though it is true that colonialism has contributed to underdevelopment, 25 years after independence, the colonial experience should cease to be a scapegoat for Africa's failure to develop. Similarly, aid has never been a solid basis for development. Development comes from the self-reliant effort of the people of a country.

Therefore the fundamental message of this book is that for Africa's development three things are necessary, namely: concrete commitment to development, not simply rhetoric; concrete effort to end dependence on the global economic system; and a people-oriented and self-reliant development strategy. To attain the two last objectives, Africa must unite and must also increase its political and economic interactions with other Third World countries. For instance, Africa could learn the lessons of autarky and self-reliance from the People's Republic of China and the Democratic People's Republic of Korea. Vietnam supplies a lesson in the fight for political-economic liberation. These are just a few examples.

This book emphasizes action. It is therefore addressed to politicians and policymakers, administrators and managers, international civil servants and general readers.

In undertaking this work I was encouraged by my former chief executive and colleague, Ibrahim M. Kaduma. My special thanks go to him. My appreciation also goes to those who, in one way or another, have contributed to the realization of this work.

Lastly, special thanks go to my wife, Hajara, for her encouragement and patience and to my children, A'isha and Rukayyatu, for their patience during the preparation of this book.

I am responsible for any errors.

1 Economic Structures, Development Theories, and Crisis

Africa is in crisis. This crisis has been going on for at least one and a half decades now, and it is customary to trace its root cause to the colonial experience. The origin of the colonial situation was capitalism and the resulting rivalry among European nations. Capitalism needed raw materials, markets, and outlets for capital, which were thus required by all those European nations pursuing the capitalist option for organizing society. Thus they divided the rest of the world into empires, which then contributed to the growth of capitalism by supplying a labor force, minerals, animals, and vegetable products. This exploitive relationship between the colonialists and the colonized has persisted up to the present in slightly different form. Today it is called neocolonialism.

The oppressive and exploitive nature of colonialism provided the African power elite with a convenient scapegoat for their failure in managing their economies efficiently after independence. It is true that colonialism was oppressive and exploitive, but it was overthrown 25 years ago. Independence, however nominal it is, has provided at least some crude options for action. The question then is: Has the African power elite acted appropriately in the interest of Africa since independence? In most cases the answer is no. It is this position that leads me to argue here that much of Africa's prevailing predicament can be explained no longer in terms of colonial experience but rather in terms of the wrong way the African power elite perceived independence and the resulting way in which they managed their economies and societies.

Africa's socioeconomic crisis has been worsening all the time. Efforts, where they have been made, to resolve the crisis do not seem to have yielded any positive results. Why? This work sets out to answer that question. Yet, in order to attempt to provide a clear answer, it becomes necessary to ask why the crisis occurred in the first place.

In Africa the 1960s were, in the main, the years of political "independence." They were the years when most African countries became nominally independent. One school of thought has described this as flag independence: beyond lowering the colonial flag and replacing it with the national flag, there is no independence. Of course, we could freely make noise, but that is the end of it. And even with respect to noisemaking, any radical noise accompanied by signs of serious action causes metropolitan powers whose interests are threatened to forestall that action. Thus real independence lies somewhere else, beyond flag independence. This somewhere else is the economy. African countries are nowhere near having a firm grip on their economies, which explains Africa's conspicuous weakness and lack of independence. The premise of my argument will become clearer in the course of these discussions.

Africa's nominal independence is reflected in a mere replacement of rulers. A set of colonial rulers along with a flag was replaced by another set of rulers along with another flag. The new rulers inherited the power and privileges of those they replaced. The colonial rulers were separated from the people by their "wizardry" and color. It was also a deliberate colonial policy to keep the rulers and the ruled apart to enable the former to exercise relatively easy control over the latter. In this way the ruled were psychologically made to accept their own inferiority along with the corresponding superiority of the rulers.

Those who replaced the colonial rulers in positions of power do not have the advantage of difference in color of skin, but they do have the advantage of their own type of "wizardry," namely, Western education. Their education, coupled with their locational separation from their people, gave them an overawing position over the rest of the society. This separation was the beginning of African crisis. The question is: How? First of all there was ignorance. Relatively few of the educated Africans at the time of independence were highly educated. Consequently most of the educated succumbed to the psychology of inferiority imposed on the populace by the colonial rulers, with the result that anything European was perceived as superior. This perception led to the effort to ape European culture and consumption patterns, which, combined with many years of schooling, set the elite apart from the people. Though members of the elite are a product of the indigenous environment, years of effort to imbibe the European way of life made them succumb to separation from their people, a separation even more acute in the case of those who came from rural areas. However, the main point of interest is the consequence of this separation as it relates to Africa's prevailing economic crisis. The consequence is clear: the ruling elite ceased to identify with the people and their problems. For this reason, development strategy was never people-oriented, and this is the crux of the matter. Development strategies were urban-biased, oriented to elitist consumption, and outward-looking. I will elaborate on this presently.

With independence came what some scholars call the tide of rising expectations on the part of the populace: they expected their new rulers, who are genetically part of them, to be more sympathethic with them; they wanted a good material standard of living in the shortest time; they were self-sufficient in food and housing, notwithstanding the quality, but they needed social services and utilities—health, water, electricity, education, roads, and so on. Their needs were very simple, their horizon limited. They did not have the opportunity to have even rudimentary education, a handicap that prevents them from enjoying the intrinsic value of education.

Education is a commodity that is not only a source of a high material standard of living but also the main source of psychological pleasure. Education is the avenue to knowledge; it is the thing that enables one to engage in enlightened debate, to know one's rights and obligations, to follow the trend in global discourse of such things as international relations, industrialization, science and technology, and space travel. Lacking education, the people are excluded from this pleasurable aspect of living.

Nonetheless, the nationalist politicians, with the bureaucratic machinery at their disposal, embarked on the effort to meet the simple needs of the people, and there was much political sense in doing so. Failure to provide in adequate quantity for these needs would threaten the existing fragile political stability. So substantial resources were allocated to the provision of social services, and, with time, such a strategy came to be associated with development.

Meanwhile the society was self-sufficient in food. Agricultural production was doing well, meeting the foreign exchange needs of the governments and the raw materials needs of the capitalist metropolitan countries. It was also meeting the cash needs of the farmers to enable them to pay their taxes and buy the few imported consumer goods they could afford. This apparent self-sufficiency in agriculture enabled the power elite to shift resources to the other sectors of the economy, namely industry and social services. I have already touched on the latter; I will now discuss the former.

The members of the power elite of those days were inevitably trained in the metropolitan countries, which gave them close contact with the advantages of industrialization. Industrialization, underpinned by science and technology, has provided the metropolitan countries with a level of material welfare unheard of in the history of human civilization. It also provided them with power supported by very strong economic bases. Since prestige follows power, industrialization also came to be associated with prestige, and African leaders were quick to appreciate this. It is assumed that they also wanted power and prestige for Africa. Hence the policy of industrialization, which started with efforts at import substitution.

While African leaders were using the same colonial economic structure to pursue industrialization and provide social services to their people, health services were improving, with the consequent fall in death rates and a rapid growth in population. The immediate effect of this rapid growth was the inadequacy of social services, a problem more acute in rapidly urbanizing areas. There were now more people and the same or fewer resources to meet their needs. At the same time agricultural production grew only marginally before the early 1970s. But more important, the value of agricultural exports was beginning to decline. There were two reasons for this: first, competition between Africa and Third World countries elsewhere producing the same commodities; and second, the development of substitutes for raw materials. The combination resulted in adverse terms of trade for Africa and consequently less foreign exchange and fewer imports of capital and consumer goods. While Africa was going through this experience, drought hit in the early 1970s. That was the straw that broke the camel's back: the immediate effect was a food crisis that has persisted until now.

The food crisis has shaken the foundations of African society. There is no need to enumerate the hardships to the people; they are common knowledge. What is more important is the manner in which this development has exposed the bankruptcy of African development strategy. It was a strategy based on a weak agricultural base, a strategy that retained intact the colonial economic structures, which had been designed to facilitate the production and export of raw materials to the metropolitan countries. No African country made any effort to build a self-generating and self-sustaining economic base. Instead, it was thought that import substitution would provide a modicum of economic independence. Import substitution failed for several reasons, namely dependence on imported raw materials and capital goods, expensive products that the general public could not afford, and orientation to the production of luxury goods, which enjoy only a tiny elitist market. Thus the illusion of independence was exposed. Africa quickly became a beggar continent crying for aid from the international community. The golden age of complacency has gone. Opportunity now challenges Africa to think hard and work hard. The reality is that there is no altruistic developer of African or indeed of any Third World countries. Hence the struggle for the liberation of Africa is yet to begin, and economic liberation is becoming the slogan at the Organization of African Unity (OAU).

Since 1984 talk of the economic liberation of Africa has been heard at the OAU. The idea is that the OAU has almost completed the political liberation of Africa, which was one of its goals at its inception in 1963; it is now time to shift the emphasis to economic liberation. It is noteworthy, however, that the distinction between the political and the economic liberation of Africa and the intention to embark on the latter struggle have come about only now, with Africa's current economic crisis. It took the deteriorated global economic situation, droughts and subsequent hunger and death, and refugees to persuade African nations that they need economic liberation. Over the past quarter of a century, it has not been understood that there could be no real political liberation without economic liberation. If the inseparability of the two had been understood, the struggles would have been undertaken simultaneously and now, twenty years later, Africa would have made some progress in its effort to attain economic freedom. Yet even the recent talk about economic liberation at the OAU seems to be mere rhetoric, for the resolve to fight for it was soon neutralized by the call for the international community to help Africa out of its present predicament. Given this kind of approach to the problem, I am sceptical about Africa's seriousness to fight the battle of economic liberation.

DEFINING ECONOMIC DEVELOPMENT

In the discussion above I have argued that Africa chose the wrong development strategy and that this explains the present economic crisis of the continent. I have argued that the choice of development strategy stemmed from lack of a clear understanding of the difference between nominal political independence and real independence, whose basis is a firm grip on the national economy. In addition, I argue that the policy of industrialization based on import substitution also results from a misunderstanding of what development is.

For this reason it becomes important to have a better understanding of what development is. Consequently this section is concerned with a discussion of the concept. However, the intention is not to provide an alternative definition; rather, it is to discuss the differently held views about development with the hope that some clarity might be attained as to what it is.

Development is a concept of wide applicability. It applies to all living and some nonliving things. With respect to nonliving things the notion of development could be applied to anything that could be improved. A good example is a technical invention. Take a machine, for example. In its first stage it may be crude and perform at less than optimum level. But with time, more knowledge, and better materials and effort, its structure may be improved, thereby improving its performance. Almost all the machines and gadgets we are using today have gone through several stages of development to attain a level at which we think no further improvement is possible.

With regard to development in living things, one could take the example of a human being. Science enables us to trace the development of the human being from conception through all the stages to maturity and decay. A similar method of study may also be applied to society. Analytical tools developed in the disciplines of the social sciences and history enable us to trace the development of societies from their origins to maturity and decay. This method of analysis has been applied especially in the history of civilizations. But in the study of societies, as in that of all other living organisms, subdivision of the organism into parts is necessary for analytical purposes. The reason for applying this technique is obvious. First, it is beyond human power to understand the whole at once. Second, knowledge is boundless and dynamic, and therefore it is impossible for an individual or a group of individuals to know everything at the same time. This weakness dooms humans to one specialization or another. It is only when the results of work in various areas of specialization are brought together that we start having some limited understanding of the whole.

For this reason the same society is studied in its various aspects by different types of specialists. For example, societies are studied in their historical, political, economic, social, and industrial aspects and an infinite number of others. It is in the same inevitable tradition that one attempts to analyze African society. I speculate about the economic development aspect of African society by asking the question: What is economic development?

It is both appropriate and useful to start with what one may call the "classical" definition of economic development. J.A. Schumpeter defines economic development as "only such changes in economic life as are not forced upon it from without but arise by its own initiative from within. . . . Every concrete process of development finally rests upon preceding development" (1978). He adds that mere growth of the economy is not development. Schumpeter then outlines key motivators of economic development, namely credit, entrepreneurs, leaders, capital, and the money market. The central element of his economic development theory is the entrepreneur. Entrepreneurs are prime movers because they have initiative, authority, and foresight and they use these attributes to bring together and combine productive factors to produce things. However, of main interest here is Schumpeter's motivators of economic development, leaders. He expatiates on leaders by discussing how they fulfill their functions—more by will, intellect, "authority," and "personal weight" than by original ideas.

Schumpeter's definition of economic development should be of special interest to Africa. Four elements of it are particularly important in understanding partially the chaotic economic situation there: (1) development is not forced from outside but arises from internal initiative; (2) the process of concrete development rests upon preceding development; (3) development is not mere economic growth; and (4) leaders are the key motivators of economic development. Let us apply these elements to the African situation.

It is well known that changes in economic life in Africa in colonial times were forced: any signs of initiative from within were brutally and sharply arrested by imperialism. With respect to this part of Schumpeter's definition, then, there has been no economic development in Africa to date. The same conclusion then applies to the second element of the definition, namely that processes of concrete development rest upon preceding development. Had there not been imperialism and colonialism, this observation would have applied to Africa. But again the preceding development was brutally disrupted, first by the slave trade and then by imperialism and colonialism.

The feudal, subsistence, and trading economies of Africa were disrupted, but they were not destroyed and supplanted by modern capitalist economies. They remained feudal, subsistence, and trading economies, but with islands of modern economic activity. This is the indefinable hybrid that the African power elite inherited.

The view that economic development is not simply economic growth is also a useful proposition in understanding the chaotic economic situation of Africa. Growth and development have been a great source of confusion there, the two terms being regarded as synonymous. The confusion has always informed the economic development strategies of Africa and will be discussed in detail later.

The fourth element in Schumpeter's definition, the role of leaders, raises the question: have African leaders applied the attributes of will, intellect, authority, and personal weight to propel the economic development of Africa? The answer is an emphatic no. Such attributes have mainly been used to suppress and oppress rather than to foster economic development. The power elite used these attributes to remain in power at all costs so as to retain the influence, prestige, and privileges that accompany power.

From what has so far been discussed concerning the definition of economic development, it is tempting to absolve the African power elite of any blame for the present adverse economic situation. There is the tendency to argue that, after all, African leaders inherited economies whose development bases had been tampered with. Changes were forced from outside, and consequently preceding development, which would have formed a foundation for further development, was distorted. It is true that the two events happened. But I will argue that the disruption of the indigenous economies was not sufficient to hinder development. There are two reasons for this argument. First, as I have already mentioned, the foundations of African economies were virtually intact, though imperialism and colonialism certainly imposed structures on these economies to facilitate the exploitation of labor and raw materials. They also initiated enclaves of "modern" economy, but the predominant structures—as feudal, subsistence, and trading economies—remained. Second, in some countries, for example, North Korea and China, development was disrupted by outsiders, Europeans and Japanese. Admittedly, the disruption was not as long as in the case of Africa. Nevertheless, the foundation for indigenous development was tampered with, and, according to Schumpeter's theory, the basis of internal and concrete development did not exist. Yet today the two countries are models of self-reliance. Why did North Korea and China succeed? They did one fundamental thing: they tried to recreate indigenous conditions necessary for success by curtailing the penetration of foreign economic influence in their societies. This is where the role of leadership becomes critical in development efforts. The leaders must have the will, the intellect, the authority, and the personal weight to lead their people to self-reliant development. Such leaders, to succeed, must be committed to the people. Even if they love power, they should love it and acquire it with the sole aim of using it to the benefit of their people. Yet at the same time they will enjoy all the fame, prestige, influence, and privileges that accompany power. And they will also be more secure and happier leaders, for they and others will witness the concrete achievements of their leadership.

Lack of clear definition of development has resulted in a great deal of confusion in the way people perceive development in Africa and perhaps in the whole of the Third World. I have discussed what could be considered a classical definition of development, the major elements of which are that: (1) development should be an internally generated change; (2) development should be based on a preceding structure; and (3) development should not be synonymous with growth. I agree with these elements, but is it a complete definition of development? In my view the answer is no. Though the classical definition is a fundamental one, I am also of the view that development should be associated with qualitative change in the conditions of living. For one fundamental goal of development is the improvement of the material condition of the people. If that is not the aim, then there will be no meaning in having a change at all. However, economic change, whether quantitative or qualitative, must be preceded by some productive capacity.

The quantity and quality of the goods and services that are intended to raise material conditions of living must emanate from some productive structures. The stronger and better-organized these are, the better and greater the quantity of goods and services produced. Productive capacity is made up of many things, but a few crucial ones may be isolated: such things as a trained and adequate labor force, highly developed structures in science, technology, and research; organization; and of course adequate and good-quality producer goods. It should be noted that in this list natural resources are not mentioned. Surely, in building up productive capacity natural resources, especially where they are abundant, are a great advantage. A good example is the United States, if not now, at least in the past. The technological lead that it has has been aided by the availability of vast quantities of resources when it began to develop. Yet there is another side to the argument as well. There are countries that have few natural resources—apart perhaps from their soils, which may be poor, and water—but have succeeded in building self-sustaining productive capacity. A good example is Japan, a highly populated country composed of islands. Agricultural land is limited and minerals are almost completely absent. Japan imports 100 percent of its uranium, nickel, and bauxite; 97.7 percent of its crude oil; 87 percent of its iron ore; 78.5 percent of its coal; 75.6 percent of its copper; and 04.6 percent of its lead. But Japan ranks among the seven industrial powers of the world, the only non-Western country to enjoy this privilege. It built a tremendous productive capacity from sheer hard thinking and hard work and with these two attributes attained economic liberation long ago. Hence the argument that natural resources are a key element in building productive capacity does not hold for Japan. Nor does it hold for the Benelux countries in Europe. There is much that Africa could learn from these countries in its struggle for economic liberation. Despite the technological gap between the two, at least one thing is clear: it is feasible to build up a self-sustaining productive capacity without a natural resource base. Perhaps such things as the will to survive, research, science and technology, and organization have a lot to do with the capacity to build productive capacity without a natural resource base. But in fact Africa has a great advantage in that it is endowed with abundant natural resources.

Perhaps Africa is the richest continent in the world at present. In addition to its fairly rich soils and abundant waters, Africa is endowed with minerals of strategic importance in industry and armaments.

It will also be observed that organization is mentioned as one of the key elements of building a productive capacity. Organization is crucial to economy, efficiency, and effectiveness. A country may be endowed with all the resources necessary for building a strong productive capacity, but it could fritter away the chance through inefficient organization. In such a situation all resources, especially manpower, are abused through either the wrong placement of experts or a proliferation of organizations. Too many organizations stretch the scanty available manpower and generate many overhead costs, most of which are unproductive. A problem of coordination is created, which again is a great drain on resources in terms of manpower, funds, materials, and time. Organizations are a critical problem in Africa. Too many are created and manpower is misused. The latter is the case especially where professional and technical cadres are looked down upon or posted to administrative duties instead of being placed where they could usefully apply their expertise.

In Africa economic development is hardly understood in terms of building productive capacity; it is understood only in terms of material well-being. But were does the material well-being come from? It comes from the productive capacity of the system. Yet in Africa economic development is synonymous with structures such as high-rise buildings, stadia, divided highways, expensive hotels, modern airports, teaching or specialist hospitals, sophisticated communications systems, television, and so on.

Though these things are associated with development, few people pause to ask: Is this type of development rooted in the needs of the populace? Is it a priority now? And where did the productive capacity that builds these structures we identify with development come from? It is clear that such things are not, by themselves alone, development. They are not the needs of the people, and the productive capacity that constructs them comes from outside Africa. Meantime we lack even the capacity to manage and maintain these relatively simple structures. We have to import managers, technical experts, and spare parts. Since we lack the capacity to manage and maintain structures built for us, it means that we are engaging in an irrelevant type of development, a type that neither is rooted in the people nor builds productive capacity.

But what are the reasons for perceiving development as described above? There seem to be two. The first mistake is in associating development solely with an improved level of material well-being and that, in turn, arises from external influences. The members of the power elite who are responsible for designing Africa's development strategies experienced a comfortable material life when they were training in the West. Naturally they came back with the desire to change their countries on the basis of the Western model of society. Hence the desire to emulate is strong. What has been forgotten is that it takes time and a lot of effort to transform backward societies into societies with a high standard of living. The second mistake is the selfishness of the power elite itself, which, accustomed to a Western life-style, finds the desire to maintain it irresistible.

Development is not just buildings, but the association of the two has brought about a curious love for structures, a malady that has permeated even the rural areas. This is seen when villagers rejoice when a modern building, whether a hospital or a school, is erected, even if it stands there for several years without being put into operation. The beautiful building may be there, but there may not be doctors, nurses, or teachers to provide the services for which it is designed. Yet governments count such things as concrete achievements simply because physical structures are visible things. But development, even if viewed solely in material terms, cannot be buildings alone. In the example just given, it is more sensible to have a makeshift or improvized structure and supply people to provide the services than to have a beautiful building that is useless because there is no manpower to provide the intended services.

Therefore development, at the initial stage, has to do with the building of the society's productive capacity. But first of all, it must be people-oriented, that is, involving the people and meeting their needs, not those of the urban elite or the external market. And to involve the people and meet their needs, their productive capacity must be built individually. They must be trained, and the tools they use in their work must be improved. Only this strategy of development offers any hope for Africa.

MEASURING ECONOMIC DEVELOPMENT

In the past, development was synonymous with growth, a synonymity responsible for the type of tools developed to measure development. I will describe these tools and point out how they have impaired understanding of development in terms of productive capacity.

In measuring economic development (progress), theories have stressed variables such as the gross national product (GNP), the gross domestic product (GDP), income per capita, population, and birth and death rates relative to the amount of wealth available to the country under consideration. However, in recent years economists have also added income distribution as a measure of economic development. This became necessary because in some countries with high GDP, the largest portion of the population still remained poor, which meant that the largest amount of wealth generated was being enjoyed by a few people. The shift of emphasis from the GDP to per capita income as a tool for measuring progress and development indicated a change in the concept of development, which now means better welfare for a greater number of people. Hence development came to be associated closely with the way income is distributed among the citizens of a country.

Let me say a few words about each of the tools of measurement in my example, starting with GDP. My definition of development emphasizes the productive capacity aspect. Could the GDP measure it? The answer is both yes and no. It is yes where the growth of GDP is associated with productive capacity. Whenever the productive capacity of an economy improves or grows, one would expect more output from the economy, thereby increasing GDP. Thus one could say that an increase in the GDP reflects a rise in the system's productive capacity and that to this extent, therefore, the GDP can measure the system's productive capacity. But the answer is also no where an increase in GDP does not reflect any concrete improvement in the economy's productive capacity. This is the case with less-developed countries (LDCs) that produce minerals and export agricultural produce. Mineral production could be stepped up without any change in the technology. When the signal to produce more comes from the market, idle capacity is reactivated to meet the demand. The rise in output is registered as an increase in the GDP, while the productive capacity of the economy actually remains the same. In this respect the increase in GDP is not a reflection of an increase in the productive capacity. The situation is similar in agricultural production. Again, the main trigger could be the market for those raw materials, or some positive development in weather conditions. When demand rises, either of two things could happen: efforts could be made to increase the supply; or, if supply could not be increased, prices would rise in response to the scarcity. In the case of LDCs supply could be increased by utilizing the idle capacity, for instance, by increasing acreage or using fertilizers. But where supply could not be increased, prices would simply rise. Both gains would be reflected in a rise in the GDP. But where there is an increase in agricultural supply, it is achieved without any improvement in technology. Similarly, in a case where demand is greater than supply and there is a resulting rise in price, this gain has nothing to do with productive capacity. Therefore in both cases the GDP registers an increase with the same productive capacity. This is the case especially in oil-producing countries where even the existing productive capacity in the oil industry comes from outside the host countries. This argument could be extended to all mineral-extracting economies.

The other tool commonly used to measure development is per capita income, the logic being that the greater the per capita income, the greater the welfare, because every individual now could obtain a greater variety and amount of goods and services. But this tool raises two problems: first, the effect of inflation on take-home income and second, the problem of distribution. Inflation has the effect of curtailing the demand for goods and services. So it seems better to have a smaller per capita income with little or no inflation than high per capita income with high inflation, which reduces welfare or at best keeps it stagnant.

Distribution presents a different problem. In situations of underdevelopment, per capita income as a tool for measuring development is merely a mathematical exercise. Certainly it tells, on paper, what each individual gets out of the aggregate national wealth, but it has two major limitations. The first is the questionable accuracy of the measure, especially in an underdeveloped context, where availability and reliability of statistics lead to a wide margin of error. Nonetheless, the tool could still serve a useful purpose, the deficiency notwithstanding. The second limitation is the extent to which it reflects actual distribution. The question here is: What percentage of the population enjoys what fraction of the national income? Per capita income is merely the national income divided by the total population; it attributes an equal amount of income to every individual. This is an ideal situation where wealth is fairly well distributed among the population, but where the distribution of wealth and income is highly skewed in favor of a small fraction of the population at the top, per capita income distribution could, in reality, only attribute statistical income to the majority of the population.

However, while the GDP is still in use as a tool for measuring the welfare aspect of development, its deficiencies notwithstanding, development theorists continued their efforts to find new tools or improve the existing ones. One new tool also measures distribution, but distribution of items such as consumption of food and nutrition per head, litres of water and milk per head, hospital beds per given population unit, and so on. In this type of measurement the central concept is access. For the distribution to be fair, access to such consumer goods and services must be made possible for the majority, otherwise this tool runs the risk of becoming a mere statistical exercise like per capita income distribution. The problem of access in a developing society is a real one. Development is urban-biased and most goods and services are concentrated in the cities, and even where such goods and services are made available in the rural areas, the meager incomes of rural people deny them access. In addition, the rural elite may simply appropriate what is available and use it to exploit the populace further.

Population is another tool for measuring the welfare aspect of development. The immediate question that arises is how to use it. Population is used in two ways: in its productive aspect and in its distributional aspect. In its productive aspect population is a factor of production—the most important one. This is especially the case where the population is well trained, but if it is large and is not well trained, in fact, it constitutes a drag on productive capacity and hence on economic progress. Yet, even where the population is well trained and productive, there is an optimum level beyond which it becomes a drag on accumulation and further development. This brings me to the question of distribution.

Developing countries are the most affected by the relationship of population and distribution. Here the population is large relative to what is produced and is growing faster than productive capacity, hence eating up whatever is produced. There is no surplus, and whatever is distributed is distributed in very small quantities. This problem has led experts to recommend the control of population growth as a solution to the vicious circle. However, this is half a solution, if it is a critical solution at all. It is hard to believe that there is any African country that has attained optimum population where available resources cannot support it. Therefore the problem is one of building productive capacity commensurate with the level of population. This is where the solution lies. The vicious circle must be broken at the level of productive capacity. This could be done in two ways. First, available resources should be managed efficiently to leave some surplus for further development. There is evidence that a lot of resources in Africa are consumed by bureaucracies, and therefore improved management could leave some surplus for investment. Second, the population should be made to work a little bit harder instead of waiting for the government to do everything for it. After all, apart from aid, governments could generate resources from the population. But again success hinges on the improvement of the equipment people use to produce. In other cases improved techniques may be available, but the problem may be dissemination or access.

There is one other aspect of population dynamics in LDCs that should be understood before one recommends any solution to the problems of economic development. Why has population growth been so rapid? The reason, which is more relevant to the past than to the present, is the question of survival of the child. In the past, chances of survival were slim, and so it made sense to have as many children as possible in the hope of having a substantial number of survivors for economic reasons. Children were an investment: they provided both labor to augment the income of the family and security for parents in their old age. However, now one aspect of population dynamics has changed and another has remained the same. Medical services have improved the chances of survival of infants and prolonged the lives of adults, with the resulting rapid population growth. But what has not changed is poverty, which in some cases has worsened. Therefore people still want children as economic assets.

The last aspect of population that I shall discuss as a tool for measuring development is more relevant to developed than to developing countries. Experts have observed that improved living conditions encourage people to have smaller families. This is a corollary of the argument I presented above. The desire to have smaller families is explained mainly by three things. First, the cost of raising children is prohibitive in developed societies. Second, time spent raising children is time that could be spent earning income. Loss of income is the opportunity cost of raising children. Third, children may constitute a drag on the quality of the parents' recreation. Population in many developed countries has now become, or nearly become, stationary, growing just enough for replacement. (The only problem is how to tackle the question of optimum population structure where the aged—nonproductive and dependent—are becoming a greater proportion of the population.) It is clear from the preceding analysis that the fundamental solution to the problem of population growth in LDCs is to raise the standard of living. This in turn can be achieved only if the productive capacity of the economy is raised.

In concluding this section, I maintain that there is a need to develop tools for measuring the productive capacity of an economy in the effort to measure economic development. Measurement should not be confined to the welfare aspect. Welfare itself is generated only by the productive base of the economy. Any measurement that neglects the economic base will neglect a fundamental aspect of measuring development and hence will not give a true picture. And perhaps the starting point for the effort is to measure energy and steel consumption and the rate of growth and application of technology. Many other variables of measurement hinging on the internal self-generating capacity of the economy could be developed.

MODELS OF ECONOMIC DEVELOPMENT

The wrong perception as to what economic development is, and the tools developed to measure it, also have their roots in the models of economic development given to the LDCs by the West. Hence the need to review these models and explain how they have failed in generating development in the Third World.

For at least a quarter of a century, a development theory focusing on growth has dominated the development strategies of the entire globe. It of course derived from the experience of the West, especially after World War II, and took root in the efforts to reconstruct the economies of the combatants. The Marshall Plan was developed by the United States, and its main strategy was the massive injection of capital into the battered economies. The strategy succeeded, and hence its transfer, even if in a modified form, to the so-called Third World countries.

When this development strategy was sold to the Third World, some factors were not taken into account, and hence its failure in most countries except those that relied on heavy debt or were clients of the West, especially of the United States, where massive aid and foreign private investment were injected. Examples are Brazil, South Korea, and Taiwan. The first relied on heavy debt for development, the price for which it is paying now in stagnation and a heavy debt burden. The other two countries are creations of the United States.

In my view three reasons explain the failure of the Western model of development in the LDCs: the weak economic structures of LDCs, lack of knowledge, and lack of oppressive instruments. I shall elaborate on each of these.

First, take the weak economic base of the LDCs. The Western countries that were aided by the Marshall Plan had strong economic bases to absorb the capital injected into them. Not so the weak and dependent economies of the LDCs. Second, the West had a long accumulation of knowledge in science and technology, which the LDCs do not have. Third, with its scientific and technological expertise the West was able to build massive war machines with which to subjugate the other parts of the world and hence exploit them. A combination of knowledge and force enabled the West to force and manipulate the Third World into subjugation and exploitation.

Thus a development theory that focused on the so-called growth center, namely factory and city, failed. It was hoped that such a strategy would generate so much GDP as to enable the masses to benefit through the "trickle-down" effect. No one paused to estimate the time dimension of the theory. It was assumed that either the GDP would be expanded quickly and the wealth trickle down fast, or that the masses would have the patience to wait for a long time or indefinitely.

The Marshall Plan model exported to the Third World emphasized the role of capital in economic development. This was in accord with the classical theory of development, which posited capital accumulation as the most important source of development. All other factors were secondary. Capital accumulation was the source of investment for industry and hence the source of growth and modernization. Industrialization generates urbanization. A school of thought came to elevate urbanization as a source of development as in the way it attracts labor from the rural areas. Yet, after some years of trial, capital, industrialization, and urbanization failed to produce development in the Third World. Too much was expected of these factors in a very short time, and they were applied in the wrong environment, one whose productive base was too weak to absorb huge doses of capital and sophisticated technology. The next question was what to do. Something was surely done, but it was merely an extension of or refinement of the conventional wisdom.

The debate then shifted to a "project" versus a "program" approach to development. The project approach was the predominant one at the earlier stages of development strategies. At the time, industrialization was chosen as a means of rapid economic development because it was thought to have the potential for building the productive base of the economy in a short time. Consequently, for some time the cost-benefit analysis approach to investment reigned. The United Nations Industrial Development Organization (UNIDO) produced a highly technical and authoritative document to this end. Yet the cost-benefit analysis and project approach did not succeed as expected. Several factors explain this failure, but the most obvious ones are the socioeconomic environment and data. A highly technical approach to project preparation such as cost-benefit analysis requires adequate and reliable data, which the environment cannot provide. Therefore, shadow pricing, in a chaotic environment, became an unreliable tool in cost-benefit analysis. This is just one of the many adverse effects of the environment. In addition, the environment cannot provide the "perfections" required of the market as it operates in developed open market economies. Moreover, the discipline to adhere to plans is also conspicuously absent because of a variety of factors, many of which are beyond the control of the developing economies.

With so many problems experienced in the project approach to development, an alternative was sought in the program approach, which emphasizes that there has to be some integration of various elements for a successful development strategy. The project approach is very much isolated from the environmental elements crucial to success. The program approach came as an improvement, along with some new thinking in development theory. In the mid-1970s experts began to propound the "redistribution with growth" and "basic needs" strategies.

Perhaps one basic explanation for this new thinking is that countries may have experienced impressive growth rates but the bulk of their populations has not partaken of the fruits of the growth. Consequently the majority of the population remained poor; Brazil is a good example. Another explanation is that a world where the majority is poor and a few are affluent constitutes a threat to global stability. Therefore, perhaps for reasons of global security, justice, and fairness, it became necessary to promote the notion of distributive equity. The debate on redistribution and growth is still not resolved; conservatives still maintain that growth should have priority, for without it there will be nothing to distribute. Meantime the basic needs approach has been refined by the World Bank (or International Bank for Reconstruction and Development—IBRD) and is presented as the main workable strategy to deal with global poverty. Though this strategy appeals to many people, there are still a few dissenting voices. There is a school of thought that believes that the basic needs approach to development is only a euphemism for discouraging Third World industrialization. However, while the debate as to the best strategy rages on, another approach is commanding new interest. This is the one of rural development, which combines some elements of both the redistribution with growth and basic needs approaches. How far the strategy of rural development has succeeded or will succeed is a moot question. More time is needed before assessment can be made.

Two other theories of development deserve mention: the Latin American dependency theory and the African center-periphery theory. These were inspired by Raul Prebisch's theory of unequal exchange between the developed countries and LDCs. Debate on these theories is still lively and is especially popular with Marxist analysts. The main theme in all these theories is the exploitive relationship between the developed and developing countries that arises from unequal relations deriving from scientific, technological, and military gaps. These theories have gone a substantial way in explaining underdevelopment.

It is also useful to look at the other side of the coin. While some were busy propounding theories of development, others were doing the same for underdevelopment. They were seeking explanations as to why Third World countries are underdeveloped. Such theories rested on limitations of the physical environment such as overpopulation, poor soils, enervating climate, and lack of natural resources; and on cultural traits such as tradition and lack of motivation for achievement. Some talked about the vicious circle of poverty to explain underdevelopment. For the most part, these theories have been discredited. As I pointed out earlier, "overpopulation" cannot explain underdevelopment. There is no convincing evidence that Third World countries are overpopulated. The main problem is that of weak productive capacity, which could be solved through efficient management of resources, the dissemination of appropriate technology, and the training of the population to raise their productivity, all of which would lead to disengagement from dependency.

And that is also how the vicious circle of poverty could be broken. As to limitations of the physical environment and cultural traits, these are hardly explanations of underdevelopment. Countries are busy making deserts bloom, and those that have few or no natural resources are using their heads and muscles to develop. And in the so-called enervating tropical climate, there are nations that are joining the ranks of the newly industrializing countries (NICs). Similarly, it is common knowledge that today cultural traits cannot explain underdevelopment. Changes in unexpected places have discredited this as an explanation. The main flaw of all these theories is that they were propounded from Western cultural bases and extol some virtue lacking in the LDCs. It was not realized that such virtues came through change and development, through socioeconomic and political dynamics. No one questioned cultural traits when the developed countries of today were backward. For instance, inventors in the sixteenth and seventeenth centuries in Europe were considered nuisances to and subverters of the established order who deserved to be suppressed. Change overthrew this destructive way of thinking; similar change will remove cultural obstacles to development in Third World countries.

After an analysis of the notions of economic development, its measurement, and some models of development, it has become obvious that Africa should have a clear understanding of the illusion of political independence. Real independence is economic. The link between a strong economic base and power and liberation should be clearly understood. And the foundation of this is a strong productive base that is internally generated and self-sustaining. Individuals and countries should be made productively strong. But as things are now, the experience of the people of Africa has been a frustrating one. Partly from ignorance and partly from bitter experience, a good proportion of the populace is even saying that the colonial situation was better. It does not know about and is not interested in sophisticated economic development models. It is interested in action and concrete results.

2 The Global Setting of the Crisis

Every morning I listen to the B.B.C. to learn the price of the cotton and coffee with which Tanzania earns its foreign exchange. The prices of tractors and other goods we need to buy are not announced; they are fixed by the manufacturers in the Developed World, and we learn what they are when we go to buy.

Julius K. Nyerere

. . . the Principle of relieving debts by increasing them.

J. H. Mensah

Such is the lot of Africa, a continent locked in an unequal exchange with the developed world. Therefore Africa, perhaps the richest continent in the world at present, has been transformed into undeniably the poorest continent. What a paradox. Africa has relatively rich soils for agricultural production. It has abundant water resources for irrigation, transportation, and hydroelectric generation. In terms of minerals it has 97 percent of world's reserves of chromium, 85 percent of its platinum, 64 percent of its gold, 50 percent of its manganese, and 25 percent of its uranium, just to mention a few examples. In short, Africa has minerals of strategic industrial and military importance.

The paradox of richness and poverty that Africa displays can surely be explained in both the global context and the domestic context, that is, in terms of the dynamics of African governments. Both contexts will be discussed, in separate chapters, in an attempt to focus sharply on the problems. This chapter is concerned with "the global context of the paradox of Africa's wealth and poverty."

The lot of Africa is to export raw materials, agricultural and minerals. Earnings from these depend on volume and price. Volume is determined by technology, prices, and the vagaries of the weather, none of which Africa has complete control over—not even the man-made institutions of technology and price.

Control over the vagaries of weather is completely ruled out. Price, on the other hand, is a function of demand and supply in the world market. And here care should be taken to note that a perfect market does not exist. The market is always manipulated by the powerful developed countries. This is especially true of monopsony, where there is a sole buyer. Techniques such as substitution and stockpiling and cutback in consumption are used to manipulate demand and hence prices. These techniques were used with respect to petroleum oil, with the resulting slump in oil prices. Meantime, it should be remembered that the Third World countries, whether exporters of raw materials or the NICs, export the same rather than complementary commodities, and so, the competition to sell is stiff. All supply the same commodities at the same time when demand is declining. The effect is obvious: oversupply and the consequent fall in prices. Again the experience of oil exporters is an obvious example.

In recent years, Africa, a continent with very fragile socioeconomic and political structures, has been facing a very harsh global economic environment. The global recession has been mainly responsible for the declining demand for the raw materials on which Africa depends for earning the foreign exchange to buy capital and consumer goods. The effect of the declining demand is a fall in the prices of raw commodities. While foreign exchange earnings are continuously dwindling, inflation in the developed countries continues unabated, and these are the markets for capital goods, which Africa needs for production and development. Hence, the unequal exchange and the adverse terms of trade for Africa and, indeed, the whole of the Third World.

While declining demand and inflation are taking their toll on Africa's terms of trade, natural disaster is adding another dimension to the problem. Droughts have been frequent and prolonged and have adversely affected production not only of export cash crops but also of food, the most important basic need. Therefore, droughts have further weakened African socioeconomic systems in two ways. First, they have drastically cut down the volume of cash crops. making it impossible for Africa to earn more foreign exchange from increased volume to offset the effect of low prices. Second, droughts have also cut food production. The result has been hunger, starvation, death, and refugee problems. This development suddenly transformed Africa into a desperate international beggar, obviously a position of great weakness. It took this disaster for Africa to appreciate the critical importance of food in the scheme of things. Everything hinges on food, for it is the key to a person's livelihood: it is food that provides energy to enable people to engage in productive activities. So, whenever an economy is able to provide its people with adequate food, then it has solved the most important economic problem. Solutions to all other economic problems become fairly easy. The importance of food in an economy should be clearly understood by African countries. Even those nations that are self-sufficient in food have still found a new use for it: they use it as a political weapon. The United States used it some years ago against Soviet Russia and perhaps several other, small countries.

Another weakness for Africa is its debt burden. Though by the standard of Latin America, Africa's debt could be dismissed as peanuts, in terms of repayment ability the debt is a very heavy burden. The most important question is the ability to repay. In Latin America the huge debtors are Mexico, Brazil, and Argentina. Evidence from various sources suggests that their economies have far stronger bases than any of those in Africa. Hence, in terms of ability to repay, they have a clear advantage over Africa. On the other hand, African economies are very weak, for reasons examined above. Countries struggling to feed their peoples cannot think about repaying debt. However, Africa should not worry now about its debt. To those who extended the credit, Africa's debt is actually very small. The most serious threat to creditors is from Latin America, where any default could cause the international banking edifice to collapse. Total Third World debt is now between $700 billion and $800 billion, a major part of which is owed to many of the largest U.S. banks. Therefore any collapse would adversely affect the domestic economy of the United States by causing a crisis.

With this background, details of the global setting of Africa's economic crisis are discussed below in three sections. The first deals with Africa's terms of trade, the second with its debt, and the third with the role of the World Bank and the International Monetary Fund (IMF) in global economic management. Most would agree with my arguments in the first two sections, but there may be some scepticism as to the relationship of Africa's terms of trade and debt to its economic problems.

There is a relationship, and it should be understood in three contexts: (1) their role in integrating Africa into the capitalist world monetary system; (2) their role in generating sociopolitical unrest in the country that accepted IMF conditions; and (3) the way this relationship influences Africa's development strategy, which is deficient. A clear understanding of the three relationships will enable Africa to appreciate clearly its dependent position in the global economic system and work toward changing the situation.

AFRICA'S TERMS OF TRADE

The issue of terms of trade has been discussed extensively and intensively following the era of commercial capitalism. As industrialization progressed, the discussion assumed greater importance for both developed and developing countries. Debate on terms of trade is still continuing, and arguments as to who is benefiting at the expense of whom will continue forever. The questions now are: Why this argument about terms of trade? What is so important about terms of trade as to generate such an amount of debate? These are the questions I want to answer in the course of this discussion.

Commercial capitalism preceded industrial capitalism. Even in self-sufficient "primitive" societies, some exchange went on. It was done by barter, but nevertheless it was a form of trade. With time, societies living far apart started to trade over long distances. But we may assume that modern commercial exchange or trade started after the discovery of distant lands by European explorers. However, of interest here is the commercial experience of Western Europe, whose countries were the colonizers of Africa. Trade between Africa and Europe started with slaves: after the abolition of the slave trade, other commodities became articles of a trade that continued for centuries until the dawn of imperialism.

As is well known, imperialism was designed to achieve specific ends: markets, sources of raw materials, and profits. As capitalism developed in the metropolitan countries, there arose competition among them for natural resources, markets, and investment opportunities. This was the reason for the partition of Africa and World Wars I and II. The European countries had relatively fewer raw materials than the other parts of the world, and markets and investment outlets at home were saturated. Yet profits and employment had to be maintained and even raised. Profits are needed for more investment and a high standard of living, and millions came to depend on external investment and trade for their jobs. Hence the rush and competition for empires. It is thus clear that the stability and survival of the metropolitan countries depended on their imperial acquisitions, with which one of the major links was trade in manufactured exports and raw materials.

When trade and exports became crucial to the survival of the imperialist countries, the theory of comparative advantage was developed. This theory maintains that nations exchanging commodities in which they have a comparative advantage will end up gaining in welfare by having from other countries those commodities that would have been more expensive for them to produce themselves. A country has a comparative advantage in a commodity it can produce at lower cost than its trading partner could. This underpins the principle of the division of labor. Going by this logic then, countries that have a comparative advantage in producing manufactures should continue to do so, as should those producing raw materials. There is one danger in this for Third World countries: countries on the periphery will never have the chance to industrialize; they will remain suppliers of raw materials. Meanwhile, countries that have a competitive advantage will continue to promote the principle of comparative advantage. But some of these strong countries were the very ones that developed their industries behind tariff walls—for example, the United States, West Germany, Canada, Australia, New Zealand, and Japan. Developing industries behind tariff walls implies a lack of comparative advantage in those industries vis-à-vis competitors. It means that goods so produced could be procured more cheaply somewhere else. Then why the tariff walls?

Why the abandonment of the principle of comparative advantage? It means there is more to trading or exporting than comparative advantage. It means there is a strong connection between industrialization and competitive advantage and power. But these are the principal nations today that depend on free trade and the virtue of comparative advantage. Therefore, the whole question of so-called free trade and the principle of comparative advantage is a subjective thing. People or countries defend it when it serves their interests; the moment it stops doing so, they abandon it. I shall presently say a few words about a glaring recent example of this abandonment when it no longer serves the purpose.

The industrialized countries enjoyed a competitive advantage in production and trade for centuries. They fixed the prices of their manufactured goods by using mark-up techniques but allowed the prices of raw materials to fluctuate to their advantage—that is, they bought them cheaply. However, as time went on, a new set of countries, the NICs, started to emerge. These threatened the competitive position of the industrialized nations in some goods and services and have a comparative advantage in items such as electronics, leather goods, textiles, shoes, rubber, and even steel and ships. But what is the result? A rise in protectionism in defiance of the economic theory of free trade and competition, which was defended for centuries. And the reasons advanced for this protectionism? Dumping of cheap goods and loss of employment from those industries that cannot compete. But this is precisely what the theory of perfect competition and the principle of comparative advantage are all about. The theory of perfect competition posits that resources should move to those activities where they can earn the highest return. This means that those industries that can no longer compete are a drain on resources. Resources should move out of them and into activities where they could be used efficiently and earn greater returns. The prevention of this movement is just one aspect of the waste arising from protectionism; the other is loss of welfare by the society subjected to protectionism. It is compelled to buy expensive goods produced locally rather than cheap imported ones.

For these two reasons there are no grounds for protectionism. All reasons such as quality, standards, and health are merely concocted to justify the practice. Thus the protectionist attitude of the industrialized countries is a glaring example of what one might call selfish economics.

Free trade and comparative advantage are no longer serving their purpose, so they are jettisoned.

These developments have heightened tensions in the world especially with respect to North-South relations. In the late 1970s there was a fleeting interest in a North-South dialogue, in which Third World countries foolishly had confidence. President Reagan of the United States killed it at Cancun in 1981. Meanwhile the West continued to push its interests through various trade negotiations. The General Agreement on Tariffs and Trade, the institution serving the industrialized countries in organizing global trade, is the one used to promote the Western position in these negotiations through manipulation and blackmail. At the same time, the United Nations Conference on Trade and Development (UNCTAD) is hardly making any progress in changing the existing structure of world trade; for example, it took 17 years for the International Cocoa Agreement to materialize. Other trade agreements with Third World countries are either facing the same delaying tactics or threatened with collapse. And the obstacles are coming from the champions of free trade and comparative advantage. This underscores the subjectivity of the theory.

There is another aspect of the application of the notion of comparative advantage that has perhaps not been adequately exposed: the industrialized countries trade mostly among themselves. They conduct some 80 percent of their trade with other industrialized nations, while the Third World conducts 80 percent of its trade with developed countries and only 20 percent with other LDCs. But what is of more interest is in what the industrialized countries trade among themselves that accounts for a figure as high as 80 percent of trade flow. They produce basically the same items with perhaps some slight differentiation in some cases (Jalee 1971). And the main consideration here may not be cheapness; it may just be efficiency in fuel consumption, for instance, in the case of cars. Or people may buy merely for prestige. Hence you may find Germany and Britain exchanging computers; the United States and France exchanging planes; Italy and West Germany exchanging cars, to mention a few examples. These examples make it clear that trade is not free, that it is an arrangement between the parties involved to exchange the same slightly differentiated products. It is a case of "We manufacture the same thing but of different shapes; get this from me and I'll get that from you." Otherwise 80 percent of trading between industrialized countries that manufacture basically the same things is inexplicable.

From the above analysis, trade, as it presently exists, means one fundamental form of exploitation. It means that the countries of the industrialized world use much of the 20 percent of their trade with the Third World to obtain raw materials, manufacture goods, and then share 80 percent of the trade in those goods among themselves.

It may be surprising that I have dwelt so long on the general practices of the prevailing world trading system instead of going to the African experience straight away. This method is adopted for one major reason: it is my belief that it is very important to understand the background and complexities of world trade to appreciate Africa's predicament clearly. With this explanation, the discussion proceeds to the African experience.

Oil and crude minerals form 40 percent of the Third World's exports, and agricultural products form 40 percent of those of most LDCs. There is no reason not to believe that Africa's position is the same. In fact, one can venture to say that, in the case of Africa, the proportions are much higher for the simple reason that it is the least industrialized and poorest continent. Africa depends on the export of raw materials for its imports of capital and consumer goods and even food. The importance of external trade and the reasons for Africa's poor performance in this sector have already been discussed. The next important step is to adduce evidence for Africa's poor performance in the terms of trade. In this respect, what do the statistics say? World Bank sources reveal that between 1980 and 1982, the prices of primary commodities, excluding oil, declined by 27 percent in current dollars. Consequently the low-income countries of Africa south of the Sahara lost income to the tune of 2.4 percent of their GDP. Another World Bank source asserts that from 1973 to 1981 low-income African countries lost 23 percent in the power of their exports to buy manufactures. At the country level, Tanzania provides a good example of this development with its terms of trade between 1980 and 1984. With 1980 as a base year, the import price index had risen to 115.2 by 1984 and the export price index to only 103.3 (Nyerere, March 20 1985). The difference is significant for poor Africa.

In 1982 the situation worsened. The import price index was 117.4 of the 1980 base, and the export price index was 95.4. Here is a clear case of transfer of resources from Tanzania to its trading partners. This trend applies, in varying degrees, to all primary produce exporters. The instability has a twofold effect: it makes it difficult to have a coherent economic policy, and it renders long-term planning meaningless. Yet the problem is that African economies need planning to develop. It is suicidal to leave everything to market forces. The fluctuations mentioned are an example of the havoc that free market forces can cause the fragile economies of Africa. And after all, people believe in a free market only insofar as it meets their needs. The task before Africa, therefore, is to break out of this entanglement of the world trading system or alternatively to gain some control over it.

DEBT AND CAPITAL FLOWS

Finance capital is the lifeblood of capitalism. And one of the reasons for creating empires was to find outlets for capital. Consequently, capital has always been and still remains the pivot of development in Western development theories. The success of capital in the Marshall Plan in rehabilitating the battered economies of the European countries gave it greater importance in development theory. The experience gained from implementing the plan persuaded its architects to transfer the model to the LDCs, where it failed because the socioeconomic environment was not taken into account. In Europe the infrastructural base and the capacity for absorbing capital existed, whereas they were absent in the LDCs. In addition there were many environmental problems peculiar to developing societies. Nevertheless, capital still remains one of the most important factors of development.

Capital is obtained in three major ways: direct private investment, loans, and grants. Grants are made by governments. Loans come from two sources, multilateral institutions such as the IBRD and the IMF, and private banks.

There are three reasons for giving loans to interested countries: profit, market, and control. Invested capital generates profit either from the production and sale of goods and services, from interest, or from both. Similarly, loans create markets for commodities and also assist in the export of goods and services through suppliers' credit. Lastly, loans enable the creditor to control the debtor to the extent of interfering with the internal affairs of the debtor country. A recent example of this is Zaire, where the IMF assumed the management of the whole economy. Such control is not limited to countries: it extends to the global trading system.

Third World countries need capital for development. However, the main problem is not internal but external capital to enable the importation of capital goods and materials for production. If adequate foreign reserves were available, this would be less of a problem because much of what is required for capital projects would be imported without recourse to debt. But foreign reserves are always scarce for reasons discussed above. Balance of payment deficits on the current account are rectified by running down reserves, attracting direct foreign private investment, or borrowing. Borrowing is where private banks and World Bank and IMF come in. In recent years the debt problem, especially in relation to Latin America and Africa, has captured the interest of the world community. Debt constitutes one of the major drawbacks to Africa's development, and consequently it must be discussed in detail.

Africa's total debt was estimated to be U.S.$170 billion in 1985 and rose over 20 percent in 11 years mainly because of high interest rates ranging from 4.1 percent in 1971 to 10.1 percent in 1981. Thirty-five sub-Saharan African countries owed $6 billion by the end of 1984, and by 1985 the amount had risen to at least $90 billion.

The debt is big enough. More important, however, is the outflow in terms of repayment. On 1982 long-term debt alone, it was estimated that sub-Saharan African countries would pay between $8 billion and $11.6 billion a year from 1985 to 1987 compared with $2.3 billion a year from 1980 to 1982. The difference is astronomical. Meantime, in 1985 and 1986, Africa sent $7 billion and $13 billion respectively in repayments, and by 1990 the figure is estimated to rise to $16–24 billion. Yet some authorities point out that these calculations have left out much in terms of arrears and short-term debts of less than twelve months. Calculations by debt experts Green and Stephany Griffith-Jonas suggest that 42 sub-Saharan African countries may be owing as much as between $130 billion and $135 billion, a figure almost double the previous calculations. This means that 35–40 percent of export earnings of sub-Saharan countries will go to service the debt, a figure 9 percent higher than in the mid-1970s. This repayment is expected in a situation where average per capita income in these countries has fallen by between 10 percent and 25 percent.

What has so far been discussed is the general situation of sub-Saharan debt. For purposes of elaboration one must look at particular examples. Zambia's difficult position was highlighted by recent riots, which resulted in deaths, because of the effort to implement conditions imposed by the IMF. In 1984 per capita gross GNP was estimated to have fallen 27 percent below that of 1974. Reserves of copper, the mainstay of the economy, are dwindling, and though it accounts for 90 percent of Zambia's export earnings, its price has fallen by 60 percent in ten years. Amid these difficulties, payments to the IMF consumed 25 percent of export earnings in 1984. There are two sources of estimates of the proportion of export earnings going to service debts in the future: Professor Reg Green, a consultant, puts the figure at 40 percent, whereas Stephanie Griffith-Jones puts it as high as 60–70 percent (*South*, July 1985). This means that, whatever the case, the proportion is unlikely to be below 40 percent, and that is big enough.

A second example is Sudan, which has a debt of $11 billion, among the highest in sub-Saharan Africa. Annual repayments are calculated at $1.150 billion over the next few years, an amount that almost equals Sudan's 1983 exports. And payments are expected when 11.5 million people, almost half the population, face starvation.

In Zaire, my third example, the country's debt was approximately $5.5 billion at the end of 1984. Like Zambia, Zaire also relies fairly heavily on copper exports, and prices have been falling. The economy has been in difficulty for the last ten years, with the crash crop sector declining by 10 percent. These are just a few of the many difficulties this very rich country faces. Yet, from 1985 to 1989, Zaire is expected to make principal and interest payments accounting for almost 50 percent of projected earnings.

Other examples come from West Africa. All West African states together owe $32 billion, which represents 30 percent of their combined GDP. Nigeria owes 30 percent of the total debt of the subregion, and this accounts for 25 percent of its GDP. For Niger, debt is 47 percent of GDP. Ghana and the Ivory Coast owe approximately $1.71 billion and $7.12 billion respectively. For many years Ghana has been bedeviled by socioeconomic and political problems, and it is only in recent years that signs of improvement have begun to appear. Yet this improvement is still at the level of reducing the size of the negative figures. For instance, the balance of payments on the current account continues to be a major problem: in 1983 and 1984 the deficits were $356 million and $305 million respectively; in 1985 and 1986, the figures were projected to be $380 million and $425 million respectively. But in 1985, one-half of Ghana's foreign exchange earnings was projected to go to debt repayment.

Like Kenya in East Africa, the Ivory Coast has always been considered the best capitalist model in West Africa. Yet it has not escaped the debt trap. Its debt equals that of Brazil in per capita terms, and in 1983 interest payments claimed more than 47 percent of export earnings. As a palliative the country sought rescheduling.

To take another example, Tanzania's economic problems started in the early 1970s when output of export crops such as sisal, cashew nuts, cotton, tobacco, and pyrethrum fell sharply. Coffee production was maintained at a reasonable level, but foreign exchange earnings still fell from $393 million in 1983–84 to $224 million in 1984–85. Meantime, political instability in Uganda, declining terms of trade, and drought brought about a 50 percent cut in Tanzania's imports and forced industries to run at between 25 and 40 percent of capacity. Commodities disappeared from the market, and the GNP declined in 1981–82 and 1982–83. This gloomy scenario notwithstanding, Tanzania had debt service obligations of $263.4 milion and $263.9 million in 1984 and 1985 respectively, claiming 25 percent of export revenue in 1984.

Table 2.1 gives both the total and the per capita debt position of 38 African countries. Perhaps the most important thing is not the size of the debt per se but the amount of outflow it generates from the very fragile and crumbling economies of Africa. Debt will increasingly claim alarming proportions of the countries' export earnings, thus effectively inhibiting recovery efforts. In this circumstance, development becomes a very distant and dim goal.

A few more words are in order about the intensity of the flow in terms of both interest rates and capital. While the average period of maturity of debt has contracted from 22 years in 1971 to 15 years in 1982, with prospects of further contraction, interest rates have risen. In 1971, Africa's average

Table 2.1
Africa's Debt Burden

Country	Total debt US $ millions	IMF share US $ millions	Debt per Capita US $
Benin	932.2	11.4	250
Botswana	530.3	–	589
Burkina Faso	697.6	11.4	107
Burundi	581.6	16.4	135
Cameroon	3320.5	30.7	357
Central African Republic	379.7	35.8	158
Chad	243.8	8.5	53
Congo	2092.3	11.1	1230
Equatorial Guinea	152.3	13.2	380
Ethiopia	2036.8	100.3	62
Gabon	1402.4	–	2003
Gambia, The	291.0	33.7	415
Ghana	1708.2	525.1	140
Guinea	1627.7	32.3	286
Guinea-Bissau	206.2	3.7	258
Ivory Coast	7107.6	648.8	799
Kenya	4169.0	428.3	230
Lesotho	244.1	4.3	175
Liberia	1148.6	237.3	574
Madagascar	2339.5	173.9	254
Malawi	1073.0	127.0	165
Mali	1392.3	84.3	196
Mauritania	1872.3	41.4	1170
Mauritius	755.0	160.7	839
Niger	1053.3	56.8	179
Nigeria	20884.5	–	230
Rwanda	436.7	10.7	79
Senegal	2540.2	234.7	423
Sierra Leone	610.0	97.6	190
Somalia	1644.2	114.3	365
Sudan	11000.0	677.7	545
Swaziland	260.4	13.5	372
Tanzania	3356.1	60.2	170
Togo	1076.1	63.5	384
Uganda	1488.8	343.9	110
Zaire	5497.2	688.4	179
Zambia	4361.7	753.8	727
Zimbabwe	2967.9	259.3	396

Source: *South*, July 1985, p. 31.

nominal interest rate was 4.2 percent, but by 1981 it had risen to 10.1 percent. And the real interest rate for all the nonoil LDCs rose to 20 percent in 1981–82 (Nyerere, 1985).

Capital flows show similar negative trends. World Bank sources reveal that private net flow to sub-Saharan Africa fell from $3.4 billion in 1980 to $1.8 billion in 1982, and projections for the 1985–87 period suggested a net outflow of $1 billion. Meanwhile, in 1981 and 1982 alone, outflows from profit amounted to 200 percent of foreign direct investment in Third World countries. Examples in concrete figures are as follows: In 1979 direct foreign investment in the Third World was $63 billion, and profits from this amounted to $140 billion. And for the United States alone, an investment of $8 billion in the Third World brought a profit of $63.7 billion in dividends, interest, branch profits, management fees, and royalties. This was so even in earlier periods. From 1970 to 1973 outflows of resources from the Third World were 3.6 times the inflows; in 1972, excluding the Organization of Petroleum Exporting Countries, it was 2.3 times; and in 1974 it was 1.6 times. The proportions may be declining but the absolute figure may be increasing. This is in addition to the fact that more capital is generated from retained earnings and borrowing within the host countries, which are erroneously classified as inflow of funds. These are the conditions under which Third World countries are expected to develop, and they are certainly harsher for Africa than for the rest of the developing world.

THE INTERNATIONAL MONETARY FUND, THE WORLD BANK, AND U.S. HEGEMONY

The World Bank and the IMF, especially the latter, are two UN institutions that have generated controversy in the world, especially in recent years, because they deal with the material welfare aspect of life. They deal with economic development, finance, and trade, which are aspects of social organization that affect the welfare of all human beings. The two institutions are the economic managers of the globe. Therefore the importance of their role in global economic affairs makes it necessary to understand their aims and operations, especially in relation to the Third World. Perhaps no UN institution has penetrated and influenced Third World systems as much as these two. They have, for years, been Third World "advisers" in economic and financial management, and in some countries the IMF has even had the clout to take over the functions of the government departments as financial managers of the host country.

A clear understanding of the aims and operations of the IBRD and IMF should start with their history. One fundamental characteristic of capitalism is keen competition. Capitalist countries or firms compete for resources and markets, a competition that led to wars and the division of the rest of the world into empires. Capitalism thrives on free trade, but whenever competition becomes very keen, protectionism grows. That was what happenned to capitalism in the 1930s, a period marked by growing protectionism, weak international capital flows, volatile exchange rates, and trade and currency wars. Free trade was threatened and a solution had to be devised. That was one of the reasons for the creation of GATT, and the IMF. Gatt was to be responsible for liberalization of trade by removing or reducing tariff and other barriers. The World Bank was to be responsible for the creation of credit to stimulate development in the Third World and thus demand for exports from the industrialized countries. The IMF was assigned the responsibility for global financial management, especially the stabilization of exchange rates.

The IMF and the IBRD were born out of the Bretton Woods Conference in 1944. They are supposed to be part of the UN system, but an analysis of their voting power and operations reveals that they are something other than that. In the IMF, which was created in 1944, each member was assigned a quota that could be altered only by a majority of 85 percent of the total votes. The United States and the major European powers obtained over 85 percent of the quotas, which meant over 85 percent of total voting power. The United States alone was allocated 36 percent, more than one-third of the total quota was paid in gold. Meantime, the U.S. dollar was tied to gold and other currencies tied to the U.S. dollar, an arrangement that gave the United States the most powerful position in the global monetary system. Even though the quota also has since been reduced, there is no evidence that it has also reduced U.S. power.

The IBRD was created in 1945 and began operations in 1946. As expected, the United States initially contributed 40 percent of the capital of the bank and therefore obtained corresponding voting strength. This has been reduced to 25 percent, but again it has hardly affected U.S. power in the bank.

I have noted the weight given to the United States and its allies on the basis of the distribution of quotas in the IMF, and I have pointed out the preponderant power obtained by the United States in the World Bank. I have also noted that, though the proportion contributed by the United States to these institutions has been reduced, this has hardly affected U.S. power in them. There are several reasons, one very obvious and important one being that the president of the IBRD is always an American. And while the managing director of the IMF is always a European, the deputy is always an American. Therefore, for all practical purposes, the two institutions are merely the extensions of the U.S. Treasury. In this respect and in many others discussed above, the IMF and IBRD cannot be genuine UN Institutions: they are U.S. or at best European-U.S. institutions.

Other possible reasons for the persistence of U.S. dominance in the two institutions are that it remains the highest contributor, that it is the host, which could give it some advantage, and that a time lag may be required before the historical preponderance of the United States declines in the minds of member countries.

The overwhelming power of the United States in the IMF and World Bank was planned. The United States had planned to surpass Europe and Britain as an industrial power, and it developed its industries behind tariff walls. It would need markets and, later, resources. To facilitate this, in turn, it had to be the champion of capitalism and free trade; hence the necessity to establish its hegemony over the world.

In its desire for hegemony the United States was aided by World Wars I and II, which fragmented Europe and weakened it both economically and politically. Meantime, the United States was far away, observing the actors destroy one another and strengthening its own economy. It did not join the wars until the later stages when the threat to its interests started to become ominous. The United States expended resources in helping to defeat the enemy, but it had never been a theater of war and thus did not experience the physical destruction of infrastructure and industry. The Soviet Union, which had been a theater of war, suffered destruction.

So, long before the end of World War II, the United States knew that it would emerge afterward as the strongest power and therefore started planning what institutions it could use and how it could use them to establish its hegemony in the world. This is the second reason for the creation of the IMF and the IBRD. Earlier, I mentioned that both were set up to ensure free trade and stabilize the world financial system. But behind this was the U.S. desire to exercise global dominance.

The next opportunity for the United States presented itself after the war, when the ruined economies of Europe needed reconstruction. Only the United States could finance it, and hence the Marshall Plan. Consequently, U.S. influence over Europe was established. However, its global dominance did not remain unchallenged for long, the first challenge coming from the Soviet Union after the Second World War. Nonetheless, the United States continued its hegemony over the capitalist world. But in the last fifteen years or so, this dominance has been challenged, for West Germany and Japan became sufficiently strong industrial powers to do so. This explains the recent persistent world crisis, but it seems to be just the beginning. The greatest challenge is an economically and politically united Europe. Europe has come a long way toward unity since the creation of the European Economic Community in 1957, but still there are major obstacles to total unity, which are nothing but rivalry over resources, markets, and trade.

The origin and aims of the IMF and IBRD show that they were established to serve the interests not of the global community, but rather of U.S. hegemony and of the Western capitalist nations. The two institutions, especially the controversial IMF, have been used as instruments of blackmail and arm-twisting, by the United States in particular, to incorporate the Third World into the global financial and trading systems. The IMF and World Bank are presented to the world as UN institutions, but the only things that connect them to the UN are the documents that established them. Their aims, operations, and power structure show that they belong to the United States, or at best to it and its European allies. It should by now be clear to the Third World that these institutions do not now and never will belong to them. Any attempt to change the power structure within them will be stoutly resisted by the vested interests. A lesson should be drawn from recent developments in the United Nations Educational, Scientific, and Cultural Organization (UNESCO) and the UN itself. The United States, Britain, West Germany, and some other industrial powers are resisting any moves toward democratization. And it is significant that this resistance is coming from those who profess democracy. Therefore there is something at stake, and it is nothing but the desire to maintain the status quo. Any democratization would reduce Western influence and the capacity to manipulate the world.

Yet, despite the fact that these institutions have been established not to benefit the Third World but to blackmail and exploit it, LDCs have a curious affinity to them. It is inexplicable how the Third World countries should be so much attached to institutions that have been established to subjugate them in a sophisticated way. The Third World has an alternative: to withdraw from these institutions and establish their own counterparts.

In fact, what is needed is one bank with two departments, one supplying long-term and the other short-term loans, counterparts of the IBRD and the IMF respectively. And when LDCs establish this bank, they should resist the temptation to dilute it, that is, to opening its doors to non–Third World nations. If they succumb to greed for aid, they will risk diluting both the goals of the bank and the means to achieve them. Once the bank is penetrated by non–Third World countries, its demise is assured. One Third World bank, namely the African Development Bank, did just that, allowing the membership of European nations. This has been brought about by greed for aid. It will be interesting to watch how the bank will continue operating. For my part, I am not confident about its smooth operation in the future.

However, let me hasten to clarify my position lest I be branded an enemy of global peace. On the contrary, I am a lover of global peace. The single most important thing that brings peace is justice. But there is no justice in the IMF and the World Bank, as I have demonstrated. If they are democratized and made genuine UN institutions, justice will have been established, and I do not see any need for a Third World bank. And the Third World cannot wait, because it is both uncertain and costly to do so.

3   The African Setting of the Crisis

In chapter 2 I discussed the international context of Africa's economic crisis; in this chapter, I deal with the African setting. The tendency has been to put the blame for the crisis on the global environment. I argue here that this is escapism. Surely, the dynamics of the international setting constitutes a problem for the progress of developing countries, but domestic constraints should not be ignored. There are usually two aspects to the problems created by the global environment, the historical and the current. In discussing the historial aspect, it is customary to blame colonialism for the ills of Africa, and there is no doubt that it distorted development. The current situation, which has prevailed for the last 13 years or so, is global stagflation, which adversely affects the external position of African countries. But 25 years after "independence," it is time for these nations to examine their domestic policies thoroughly to see whether they have not been more responsible for the predicament than external factors.

In fact, I argue here that domestic factors have been more responsible for the problem than external ones. There has been a lot of complacency over the years. Africa is richly endowed with all sorts of resources, but management has been very poor. There has been too much dependence on the external sector of the economy. There is no convincing evidence that policies were initiated and pursued to reduce this external dependence. And even where they were, they have not lasted long because policies are changed even before they are even clearly understood by the populace, let alone taking root in the socioeconomic and political environment. Economic development is a long-term business, and it requires patience and sacrifice.

This chapter is divided into three sections, dealing with problems of production, of welfare, and of policy and management. Details of the crisis will be discussed in order to bring out the gravity of the situation, and statistics will be used as much as possible. Most of my views on these problems will be devoted to the third section.

PROBLEMS OF PRODUCTION

Let us first see Africa in the global context again. In 1979, Africa's per capita income was estimated to be $700.00, and the growth between 1970 and 1979, was 1.1 percent. The per capita income was second last to that of Asia ($310.00), but Asia's growth rate of 3.0 percent was very impressive, being the highest of all the continents. In terms of growth, Africa shares last place with Central America.

Secondly, a comparison of the regions in terms of per capita GDP growth from 1980 to 1985 reveals further the plight of sub-Saharan Africa. While Asia, industrialized countries in North America and Japan, and Europe recorded growth of 19, 9, and 7 percent respectively, sub-Saharan Africa registered a negative growth of − 7 percent (table 3.1) as compared to − 11 percent recorded by the whole continent. Of course, the Middle East had the highest growth of − 20 percent, understandably, because much of the region depends on oil as the sole engine of growth. With the collapse of the oil market, a sharp decline in growth is the obvious concomitant. This is worsened by the political instability of the region. On the other hand, Asia's performance shows that all other developing regions of the world have a lot to learn from it about the "secrets" of growth in this period of global stagnation.

Table 3.1
Growth of Per Capita GDP 1980–1985

Category/Region	Percent
Industrial countries	9
Developing countries	–
Africa	-11
of which, sub-Saharan	− 7
Asia	19
Europe	7
Middle East	-20
Western Hemisphere	− 7

Source: IMF, *World Economic Outlook*, April 1986.

There are three possible reasons for the poor performance in growth. One is the dynamics of the global economy, which has been more or less on the decline. The poor performance in growth is a consequence of the openness of African economies. The second reason is the natural disasters experienced by African countries for several years. The third, which is applicable only to some African countries, is political instability, for example in Southern and Northeastern African countries such as Ethiopia, Somalia, Sudan, and Uganda. And though Africa occupied second to last position in per capita GNP with $700.00 in 1979, new statistics show that the figure had in fact declined to $500.00 by 1985. And there is hardly any sign of reversal of the trend. The reasons for this development are well known and need not be repeated here.

In another dimension, a study of 68 LDCs revealed that 1.34 billion of 2 billion people live in rural areas. There is evidence that Africa has more rural population than any other continent in the world. If economically active agricultural population is a measure of rural population, then Africa's agricultural population of 65.4 percent in 1980 makes it the continent with the highest rural population (table 3.2). With growth declining, and hence the incidence of poverty increasing, there is no cause for hoping that the figure of 65.4 percent has fallen significantly downward by 1986. In all continents the rural dwellers are the most disadvantaged in development and welfare. The conclusion with respect to Africa is then clear: it has the highest rural population and hence the highest incidence of poverty. In addition, 117 LDCs will be unable to feed themselves by the year 2000 if they continue to use the present farming technologies. Where is agricultural technology poorer than in Africa?

Detailed statistics paint a gloomier picture for Africa. Landlessness is growing. Between 1968 and 1980 the average rate of decline in the amount of land per capita was 0.8 percent per year. Between 1970 and 1980 it was 12 percent. And at the country level, Kenya is experiencing an alarming increase in landlessness at a rate of 5 percent a year. These developments look alarming, and it is tempting to blame them and the production problems associated with them on population growth. There is no doubt that population growth is a reality, but production problems are different; they are technological problems. Much more densely populated countries have been feeding themselves ever since the Green Revolution. Therefore the arguments of population growth and declining land per capita cannot adequately explain the problems of agricultural production in Africa. Nonetheless, of 83 countries studied by the Food and Agriculture Organization (FAO), 21 had a negative growth rate from 1968 to 1981, and 15 percent of these are in Africa. Africa has 26 of the least developed countries, and 28 countries have a food crisis. The problems are many. Those outlined above are only

Table 3.2
Population (millions)

Continent	Year	Average Annual Growth rate(%) 1970-80	Total	Agric-Cultural	Total	Economically Agric.	Active % in Agric.
Europe	1970		460	92	202	42	20.8
		0.5					
	1980		484	71	217	32	15.2
North America	1970		226	9	96	4	4.2
		0.8					
	1980		246	6	111	3	2.7
South America	1970		190	74	61	23	38.1
		3.0					
	1980		245	79	78	25	31.7
Central America	1970		93	42	28	13	46.4
		3.3					
	1980		124	47	39	15	38.5
Africa	1970		355	246	138	99	71.5
		3.2					
	1980		470	298	174	114	63.4
Asia	1970		2091	1359	889	577	64.9
		2.2					
	1980		2557	1487	1052	608	57.8

Source: *FAO Production Yearbook*, 1980 (Rome, FAO).

the general ones. Let us come down to specifics, namely problems of agricultural production.

The problems of agricultural production are again of two types, general and specific. General problems have to do with policy orientation, whereas the specific ones have to do with details of agricultural production at the level of policy implementation. There are five problems at the general level: (1) production geared toward international and urban demand and tastes; (2) orientation of consumption to food grains; (3) adoption of mechanization that is very energy-intensive and in some cases unsuitable for tropical conditions; (4) adoption of sophisticated technology in agricultural and other types of production; and (5) political instability in some subregions of Africa. Similarly, there are also five specific production problems: (1) over-reliance on rain-fed agriculture; (2) low investment; (3) wrong agricultural policies; (4) inadequate institutional arrangements (for example, low pricing, storage and marketing problems, and inadequate and poor dissemination of research); and (5) inadequate or inappropriate financial intermediation. The main solutions to these problems usually proposed are also five in number: (1) inward-oriented production policies; (2) emphasis on smallholder production and simple and appropriate technology; (3) expansion of research and extension activities; (4) provision of good incentive structures; and (5) the use of irrigation and quick-yielding varieties. Thus it may be observed that the problem of production in Africa is mainly that of policy and management, for the simple reason that the problems and their solutions are well known. This argument will be amplified in the third section of this chapter.

Disasters have added another dimension to the production problem. An example is a drought that lasted from 1973 into 1974, the immediate effect of which was hunger and famine—but this is common knowledge and does not need further recounting.

Perhaps to appreciate further the plight of Africa's economy the reader needs a few more statistics. I am aware that statistics have been quoted many times and at a different levels, yet I will risk boring the reader with some that have been recycled many times in various forums. It is the fashion. If one writes a paper or gives a lecture without quoting statistics, one's effort will be dismissed as unacademic, substandard, or unsupported.

It is appropriate to start with the statistics for the GDP. In 1983, Africa's GDP declined by 1.3 percent; in 1984 it increased by only 0.2 percent. But from 1980 to 1984 it declined by 10 percent. There may have been a marginal increase in 1985 owing to good weather and the consequent good harvest. But any increment that is not higher than the average population growth of about 3 percent will be recorded as negative or at best stationary.

In agriculture the statistics are as gloomy, if not gloomier. Two aspects of agriculture are important, general agricultural production and food production. The reason is simple: agriculture is the mainstay of Africa's economy, and the food crisis is the immediate problem facing the continent. Considering the two aspects will sharpen understanding.

In general agricultural production let us first consider gross performance. In the 1960s agricultural production per capita grew by 2.6 percent, but population also grew at the same rate, and the net result was no growth at all. The situation worsened in 1971–1981, when the average annual growth rate of agricultural production was 1.7 percent, but per capita growth rate was 1.2 percent. In 1980–83 the average annual growth rate of agriculture was 2.1 percent, but per capita it was −1.6 percent. And, taking 1983 alone and by subregions, agricultural production declined by 7.2 percent and 3.8 percent in West and Southern Africa respectively. In terms of value added, in 1983 agriculture declined by 0.5 percent and in 1984 by 0.1 percent. On the whole, gross agricultural output sank to the 1982 level.

With respect to food production, in the 1960s, self-sufficiency was 98 percent; now it is 86 percent. In fact, an Economic Commission for Africa (ECA) source reveals that between 1978 and 1980, food self-sufficiency was at 71 percent. The details are as follows: in 1971–81 average annual growth rate of food production was 1.8 percent, but per capita it was −1.1 percent; and in

1980–83 respective the figures were 2.1 percent and −0.9 percent. In 1983 alone, food production declined by 3.1 percent compared with 1982. By subregions the declines were 7.4 percent and 4.1 percent for West and Southern Africa respectively. But there is also an important irony to this situation. While food production has been declining in the 1980s (table 3.3), in 1984 cash crops such as coffee, cocoa, cotton, and tea did well. This was the year when the economies of the industrialized countries picked up, and the coincidental rise reflects the dependent nature of African economies.

Enough has been said about the performance of African economies, especially the agricultural sector. The question now is: What does this show about Africa and what are the immediate consequences for the continent? It

Table 3.3
Indices of Production 1980–1983 (1976–1978 = 100)

Africa South of the Sahara	Food		Agriculture	
	Net	per cap.	Net	per cap.
1980	109.44	94.50	108.93	94.04
1981	110.52	92.57	110.10	92.21
1982	114.45	92.79	113.68	92.33
1983	114.99	90.57	114.45	90.13
Northern Africa				
1980	106.94	93.58	106.52	93.18
1981	113.07	96.36	110.76	94.18
1982	111.23	92.36	109.76	91.09
1983	115.80	93.69	113.82	92.05

Source: Extracted from *Monitoring the Implementation of the Agricultural Part of the Lagos Plan of Action* (Rome: FAO, 1984), Appendix A.

demonstrates that Africa is complacent and heavily dependent on the global economic system. As to consequences, there are several. The immediate one is, of course, hunger, starvation, and death, which have attracted the attention of the international community. For this reason, between 1970 and 1980, Africa's food imports grew at an alarming rate of 8.4 percent. And by the 1980s approximately U.S. $5 billion had been spent by African countries on food imports (Tipoteh 1985). It is also important to note the structure of the food imports: 80 percent of them were wheat and rice for the urban population. Other consequences for African countries of the poor performance of their economies are that 16 of the 25 poorest countries in the world are in Africa; that an estimated 60–65 percent of the African population is poor; and that, of those, 90 percent live in rural areas. In 1968–81, of 21 countries that registered negative growth rates, 15 were African. It is estimated that nearly three-quarters of the world's poor are in 8 countries, three of which are in Africa.

Various official reports have documented a sharp rise in food imports in several countries so as to avert famine. In West Africa, Nigeria is a typical example: in 1982 its food imports peaked at N2 billion (N1 = U.S. $1.44 then). Similarly, for several years Ghana, Mali, Niger, and other nations survived on food imports or aid. And in Southern Africa, Zambia and Mozambique have been net importers of food in recent years, while Botswana has, to some extent, survived on food aid. The same applies to Tanzania in East Africa and to Kenya in the 1984–85 season. There are so many countries that survive on imported food. Those that lack foreign exchange to do so rely on aid.

The preceding discussions about Africa's production problems are at a regional level. It is also useful to look at examples at a subregional and national level, where appropriate. In this regard, the Southern Africa Development Coordination Committee (SADCC) region and Tanzania will be discussed.

Some countries in the SADCC region depend on agriculture for over 90 percent of their merchandise exports. However, the region has been self-sufficient in food since 1965. But by 1980 self-sufficiency had dropped to 80 percent, a gap of 20 percent. On average, from 1979 to 1981, one-fifth of this gap was supplied from imports for consumption (FAO 1984). And one-third of these imports was food aid. In food, aid constituted 40 percent of total cereal imports. The quantity of food aid seems to be growing. The fear now is that it may encourage a shift in consumption to high-technology foods such as wheat and rice, which, apart from being a disincentive to local production, promotes or sustains outward-looking production policies that have been detrimental to Africa's development since independence.

Let us trace the declining performance in SADCC agriculture. The growth rate of food fell from 2.4 percent to 1.7 percent from the 1960s to the 1970s. The growth rate of exports also fell, from 0.40 percent in the late 1960s to −0.4 percent in the 1970s (1984). Total annual cereal production was estimated by the FAO to be 9.3 million tons in 1981; it declined to 8.3 million in 1982 and 7.3 million in 1983. Meantime, food aid shipments also fluctuated with production. In 1981–82 shipments were 765,000 tons; in 1982–83 they were 522,000 tons following the decline in domestic production. But historically, food aid grew from 20,000–40,000 tons of cereals in the early 1970s to an estimated 1 million tons in 1983–84. This was happening when post-harvest losses from pests and diseases were estimated to be 30–40 percent or even more. In absolute terms, these losses are estimated to be 2 million tons a year (1984), ahead of food imports by a wide margin. This strange situation, which is a reflection of complacency, is not confined to the countries of the SADCC region. Almost all African countries are culprits, losing food easily and turning themselves into international beggers for food and all sorts of aid.

Tanzania is an example of a nation with production problems. Though located in East Africa, it is a member of SADCC as well as the Frontline States. Real per capita income declined by 11 percent in 1985 as compared with 1980. Like many other African countries, Tanzania relies very much on cash crops to earn foreign exchange. But in 1985–86 cash crop purchases declined by 28.6 percent, occasioning a decline in export earnings of 22 percent.

And because of this decline in agricultural production the worst has been happening in industry. Industrial production declined for six consecutive years up to 1985. In 1985 it declined 6.4 percent as compared with 1.3 percent in 1984. The contribution of industry to GDP followed the same trend, falling by 10 percent in 1982. In 1983 the fall was 8.2 percent, and generally industry operated at 30 percent below capacity. In discussing agricultural production, two aspects are usually not given adequate attention. These are livestock and forestry. Yet much of the resources of Africa consist of these. Therefore I will deal with forestry here. Livestock cannot be discussed because of insufficient data and information.

Forests play an important role as providers of resources and employment, and I will discuss the former as it relates to production. The resources provided by forests are of two types, direct and indirect. Those provided directly are food (fruits) fodder for animals, medicines, wood for fuel, poles for the construction of dwellings, and timber for industrial use. And those provided indirectly are nutrients to soil (nitrogen fixation, organic fertilizers), prevention of soil erosion, stabilization of sand dunes, shelterbelts to arrest desertification, a hospitable environment for animals (game meat), and stability of water flows.

Of the direct resources of forests, I want to discuss one, namely firewood, in greater detail because it is a great rural need whose supply and demand situation has reached a crisis point especially in the Sahel region of Africa and in urban vicinities. The reasons for this crisis are manifold. First, the growth of population causes a rise in demand for energy for a variety of uses. Second, the rising demand for food, again because of population increase, has in turn generated greater demand for land for cultivation at the expense of the forests that provided firewood. Third, there is the demand for land by the plantation industry. Fourth, grazing and increased farm acreages here continuously degraded and diminished forest resources.

A few statistics underscore the seriousness of the firewood situation in LDCs. Eighty percent of wood removed from forests in developing countries is used for fuel or charcoal. In rural areas, wood accounts for 90–98 percent of energy consumption. Nine out of ten people depend on wood for fuel. And nine tenths of the wood taken from forests is used for fuel. For these reasons the demand for firewood is growing by 5 percent annually, and shortages affect at least 230 million people in West and East Africa. Consequently, forests are disappearing at the rate of 0.6 percent a year. These few statistics show that firewood is a critical rural need and hence reflect the importance of forests to rural life. A large literature has been produced on firewood, perhaps because it benefits mankind directly. On the other hand, there has not been as much emphasis on the indirect benefits or resources provided by forests.

The indirect benefits of forests are generally those of soil stabilization through a variety of ways such as the provision of organic fertilizers, arrest of desertification and movement of sand dunes, and preservation of water courses. These improve soils for high agricultural yields and provide an ecological balance for other creatures, such as the animals useful to humanity, to flourish. And since food is now the most serious problem in the LDCs, and especially in the rural areas, the importance of indirect benefits provided by forests cannot be overemphasized.

However, their usefulness to mankind notwithstanding, forests are being mismanaged. In recent decades there has been rapid increase in human population. Improved veterinary services may also have contributed to the increase in the population of domesticated animals. Consequently, the demand for land for a variety of uses such as food and fodder production, grazing, commercial plantations, urban projects, and industrial and development projects such as dams, roads, and communications establishments has correspondingly risen.

Similarly, as was noted earlier, the growth in population led to a corresponding growth of demand for firewood. The combined effect of these factors is the removal of forest cover and the consequent degradation of the environment. The results are obvious: soil erosion (by wind and water), flooding, siltation, and desertification, to mention the major ones. The ultimate effect is a decline in soil fertility, which, in turn, leads to decline in food and fodder production and supply of firewood. A decline in food and fodder production occasions famine, while a decline in the supply of wood for fuel occasions loss of output and income directly and indirectly through the expenditure of more labor time to fetch it from long distances.

Again take the SADCC as an example. In this subregion, 70 percent of all energy consumed and 90 percent of rural household energy comes from wood. Demand for wood is expected to double by the year 2000. Afforestation programs are progressing with 20,000 hectares costing $20–30 million a year. However, as in other parts of Africa, the populace perceives forests as a free resource and hence fails to understand the benefits of conservation to themselves and society as a whole. To change this attitude will take time, but surely the first step is to involve the people in forestry programs, to tap their local knowledge, and to win their confidence.

However, it is noteworthy that some countries are making efforts to manage their forests economically. Sudan and Tanzania are good examples. The latter has had a big forest program for many years, but the former has the biggest program in the region. In Sudan a shelterbelt project against desert encroachment undertaken in the northern province has succeeded in reducing wind speeds by 30 percent and evaporation by 25 percent, while soil temperatures and air humidity have increased and sand dune movements have been checked. But this success notwithstanding, a major problem, maintenance, remains. Villagers and nomads usually regard shelterbelts as government property to be used for fuel, a situation that underscores the need to involve and educate the people in designing forestry programs and projects.

THE WELFARE PROBLEM

By welfare I mean access to good nutrition, health, education, good water supply, and similar services, for these contribute to a healthy and productive material wellbeing and life in general. In the following discussions, I will use several indicators to measure how well or otherwise Africa is doing in welfare. These indicators are food intake and nutrition, life expectancy, literacy, and infant and child mortality. One other important indicator, water, is usually ignored in most discussions of welfare. First, water is crucial to life; nothing happens without it. We use it for drinking, cooking, washing, irrigation and gardening, and even industrially. For poor populations, especially those who live in the desert, water is invaluable. Second, water has a close connection with health. It is common knowledge that clean water enhances health, whereas dirty water does the opposite; therefore, for the purposes of preventive health service, clean water is crucial. Yet when welfare indicators are discussed, in relation to health, the emphasis is on the death rate, infant mortality, the incidence of malaria, and the like, and access to clean water is relegated to the background. Unfortunately, however, the water supply situation in Africa cannot be discussed here because such data and information are not available.

The first important indicator of welfare is calorie intake and nutrition. The two go together, for it is not merely the quantity that matters; quality does also. The poor nutritional situation of Africa is implied even at the general level of poverty. For instance, taking the years 1975–80 as the base period, Africa had the highest proportion of high-poverty countries in the world—16 out of 25. In the period 1970–80, one-third of African countries had negative growth in nutrition, and only one-quarter had marginal improvement. Twenty-five countries have what the FAO describes as a high-risk nutrition problem, that is, less than 95 percent of calorie requirements are met. Meantime, only 7 countries significantly improved (by 5 percent or more) in calorie supply over the 1970–80 period. But among these, Algeria, Lesotho, Mauritania, and Botswana depended heavily on food imports to attain the improvement. In fact, the last three of these countries received food aid. Only Rwanda improved its nutritional status without depending much on imports or food aid.

Food aid has been a major way of relieving Africa's food problem, and unfortunately this palliative grew in importance between 1971 and 1980. And given the period of drought between 1980 and 1985, food aid cannot be said to have declined. On the contrary, one would expect it to be increasing. But, when Africa was doing well in food production, it received only 6 percent of global food aid to LDCs. Now it receives at least 50 percent of food aid and thus replaces Asia as the world's principal recipient. This is not surprising when one looks at table 3.4. With respect to the three indicators of nutrition, life expectancy, and literacy, again table 3.4 is a good summary of the situation.

Africa is worse off than any other continent in terms of its child death rate and infant mortality (table 3.5). Of the 41 African countries studied, 31 have a child death rate of over 20 per 1,000, and 37 have an infant mortality rate of 100 per 1,000. This situation is clearer when Africa is compared with other regions of the world. Table 3.5 reveals that, in child death rate, Africa

Table 3.4
Undernutrition, Life Expectancy and Illiteracy by Region

Region	Number of countries	Undernourished Millions	Undernourished % of total Population	Life Expectancy At birth simple average years	Illiteracy age 15 and above Millions	Illiteracy age 15 and above Percent of Population 15 and above
Africa	37	72	19.6	49.3	130	64.7
Latin America	24	41	11.3	65.2	44	20.5
Near East	14	19	8.9	55.7	66	53.9
Asia & Far East	15	303	23.1	56.0	370	48.3

Source: Rural Poverty in Developing Countries and Means of Poverty Alleviation (Rome: FAO, 1982).

Table 3.5

Distribution of Countries by Child Death Rate and Infant Mortality Rate of Regions, Average for 1968–1980 (number of countries)

Level of the Indicator	Africa	Central Latin America	Far East and Oceanic	Near East	All Countries
Child Death Rate (Per 1000):					
High (30 and over)	16	Nil	Nil	2	18
Medium High (20 – 29)	15	2	5	3	25
Medium (10–19)	8	5	4	4	21
Low (Below 10)	2	17	9	8	36
Infant Mortality Rate (Per 1000):					
High (150 & over)	15	Nil	3	2	20
Medium High (100 to 149)	22	5	6	6	39
Medium (50 to 99)	3	8	5	6	22
Low (Below 50)	1	11	4	3	19
Total	41	24	18	17	100

Source: How Development Strategies Benefit the Rural Poor (Rome: FAO, 1984).

47

always has countries concentrated in the high and medium high categories; it also has 16 of the 18 in the high and 15 of the 25 in the medium high category. The trend is the same for infant mortality. The table speaks for itself.

PROBLEMS OF POLICY AND MANAGEMENT

The last major explanation of Africa's economic crisis is policy and management. There are as many examples of these problems as there are African countries. Consequently this problem can only be discussed at the continental level. For this reason, the discussion starts with the performance of the Lagos Plan of Action (LPA) and the reaction to this of the heads of state and government.

Five years after the LPA, the heads of state and government observed that its implementation had been far below expectation. Consequently, at their session in Addis Ababa, 18–20 July 1985, they passed the Declaration on the Economic Situation of Africa, in which they resolved to have well-formulated development strategies and plans committed to a gradual increase in the share of agriculture in total national public investment to between 20 percent and 25 percent by 1989. The declaration was followed in June 1986 by the African Program for Economic Recovery, costing U.S. $128 billion, endorsed by the UN General Assembly. From this declaration, it does seem that there is commitment to sustain the momentum. Let us hope that the same obtains at the national level.

One basic problem in Africa's economic crisis is policy. This is a very important problem, but the importance derives as well from political commitment. The importance of policy lies not merely in terms of shift of emphasis to agriculture and rural development or from outward-looking to inward-looking development strategy, but also in what I wish to call durability. Policies of African governments seem to be characterized by rapid change and consequent inconsistencies and hence are marked by lack of clearly defined long-term goals. Instead, Africa operates by plodding on from day to day, improvising, with chaos and confusion as the result.

If Africa has an operational style marked by lack of clearly defined long-term goals and direction and by chaos and confusion, there must be reasons for that. What are they? There are several. The first is perhaps the desire to transform African societies on the Western model by adopting the lifestyle of Western societies. And it does seem that those who genuinely wish to improve the standard of living of the populace and do not look to the Western model are few in number. The second reason for the chaos and confusion is, I think, competition for power. People like to attain and retain power by all means, and therefore a lot of time and other resources are dissipated in competing for it. Power confers control over people and resources and brings infinite privileges, benefits, and contentment for all power-wielders, with very few exceptions.

Third, there are also those who enjoy chaos or confusion for ulterior motives, expecially material ones. A chaotic environment allows them to deploy resources in dubious ways without running the risk of being detected because of the diversion afforded by the chaos.

The fourth reason, which is related to the first and where there is genuine desire for development, is the attempt to do too much too fast. Let us take an example. The World Bank's "World Development Report" 1985, on the subject of aid with respect to project lending, points out that "Kenya in the early 1980s was trying to cope with 600 projects from sixty donors" (107). Similarly, the United Nations Development Program has estimated that there were 188 projects from 5 donors in Malawi; 321 projects from 61 donors in Lesotho, and 614 projects from 69 donors in Zambia. The chaotic policy environment has two major adverse results: the lack of durability of policies and in consequence, lack of concentration of development efforts. In this environment policies are so fragile, lacking regularity and consistency, and changed with such rapidity because of impatience and a deluge of ideas from external sources.

Policies are changed even before they are clearly understood and start taking root in the system. The major consequence is that whatever resources are available are stretched over too many projects and result in waste and unattainability of targets or objectives. In this hurry it is forgotten that development and change need patience and time in addition to physical resources. For this reason it makes a lot of sense to have a few fundamental policies and a tenacity of purpose.

The other major problem of Africa's economic crisis is management, by which I here mean public administration. Again, the importance of management derives from political will and policy. If both give management the priority it deserves and maintain that priority, then Africa's economic crisis will be solved without much difficulty.

Yet management, like political will and policy, has suffered serious neglect as a tool of development. Management of development is a difficult art. It can be viewed in both broad and narrow perspectives. In its broad perspective, it entails a close interaction with policy in terms of how they impinge on and bring about change in each other. In its narrow perspective, management is strictly viewed in terms of implementation of programs and projects and the smallest and most detailed activity. In short, in this perspective, management does an executive job.

Africa's economic recovery program needs three initial things more than anything else: improvement, rehabilitation, and maintenance of existing development structures including management structures themselves—that is, management should reexamine itself with a view to eliminating its deficiencies.

The deficiencies of African management are many, but I will discuss only three that I consider of greater importance than the others. These are: (1) emphasis on money and machines as tools of management; (2) emphasis on manpower training as against the structure and number and size of organizations; and (3) emphasis on central administrative services and procedures as against field action.

In the area of emphasis on money and machines as tools of development, management measures itself by the size of expenditure incurred in implementing programs and projects, not by the number implemented so far relative to costs, or the stage of implementation relative to costs, or the impact of the implemented projects on the target group or community or on society in general. A similar mentality is associated with machines: capital-intensity is considered prestigious, and consequently machines are valued more than human beings. Hence the desire for mechanization without consideration of the adverse impact on employment, appropriate technology, and the problems of poor maintenance capability. There is much more to say, but I think these two observations suffice.

The second deficiency of management is its emphasis on manpower training to the detriment of the rationalization of organizations. I am not denying the importance of manpower training as a solution to management constraints. In fact, manpower is most important in the management of development. Yet the other aspect of management, namely utilization, should not be neglected, for it results in cost-effectiveness and efficiency and the consequent savings.

It is well known that misuse of manpower is common among governments: too many people do too few things. Bureaucracies keep bulging; organizations keep proliferating; every new program or project has to have its organization in order to acquire some semblance of importance. The consequences are huge expenditure on maintaining ever expanding bureaucracies and the creation of coordination problems, which cost time and other resources.

The third deficiency of management is the emphasis given to central administrative services and procedures as against field action. The two adverse consequences are the wastage of resources and time on unnecessary administrative services and procedures and the slow and cumbersome implementation of projects in the field. Let us examine a few examples of resources wasted on cumbersome administration.

In the global program to combat desertification, 80 percent of investment resources went to supportive or administrative activities, with the meager balance going to the more crucial field work. But the problem is most serious in Africa, as is shown clearly when its performance in cost-effective administration in the agricultural sector alone is compared with that of Asia and Latin America. In the 1980s it is estimated that while Africa spent 37.8 percent on administration, Asia and Latin America spent only 2.6 and 11.5 percent respectively.

Within Africa itself, the proportions are more revealing. In the same period, taking the agricultural sector, when Africa spent 37.8 percent on administration, it spent a meager 4.9 percent on training and 5.3 percent on research. And at the country level, Ghana affords a good illustration. In 1969, Ghana allocated c (cedis) 25.6 million to agriculture, but over c 21 million went to recurrent costs, leaving a meager c 4.5 million for capital expenditure. Recurrent costs then represent 82 percent of the budget. Five years later the situation had not changed very much: the total agricultural budget was c 51.9 million; recurrent expenditure was allocated c 35.5 million; and the balance of c 16.4 million went to investment expenditure. Recurrent allocation was still 68.4 percent of the total budget.

From the above deficiencies, the importance of management in development becomes clear. There is no dearth of programs and projects for management to implement; what is conspicuously lacking is field action. Field action requires decentralization of decision making, not merely of administrative structures. It also requires the rationalization of administrative structures. It needs the curtailment of bureaucratic growth.

4   OAU Strategies to Resolve the Crisis

We the countries of the Third World, are thus being forced to face up to
another reality; that while we are weak separately, we could have
strength if we acted in unity.

Julius K. Nyerere

The painful and humiliating fact is . . . that African states stand firm to
demonstrate solidarity in word rather than in deeds.

Ide Oumerou

The African socioeconomic crisis and its dimensions are common knowledge. It has been extensively and intensively researched, and many reports
have been written and extensive discussions have taken place—and they are
still taking place. All this implies that the solutions to Africa's problems are
also well known. And it is also my view that, relative to both Africa's present level of development and its needs, resources are available. There is no
dearth of things to do. But with all these advantages, what is happening to
the crisis? What is being done? What are the solutions being put forward to
deal with the crisis? Why does it seem to defy solution? African governments have been battling the crisis for over ten years, but the situation
seems to be worsening instead of improving.

In this chapter I want to examine these questions with a view to finding
explanations. My opinion is that there are two major explanations, which I
will examine in detail below. These are a lack of political will and an emphasis on externally derived and oriented solutions. The proposed solutions
to the crisis are categorized into two types, namely internally and externally
derived and oriented solutions.

INTERNAL SOLUTIONS

Concern about the socioeconomic predicament of Africa was perhaps first shown in the Monrovia Strategy for the Economic, Social, and Cultural Development of Africa, the forerunner of the LPA, whose main ideas and strategy were articulated in April 1980. As far as African countries are concerned, the LPA is a very important strategy for the economic development. Therefore it is useful to examine at least a few of its important parts.

The opening of the preamble to the LPA resolution is very significant, at least in terms of rhetoric, and therefore needs quoting:

Africa's almost total reliance on the export of raw materials must change. . . . Africa must, therefore, map out its own strategy for development and must vigorously pursue its implementation. . . . Africa must cultivate the virtue of self-reliance [and] efforts toward African economic integration in order to create a continent-wide framework for the much needed economic co-operation for development based on collective self-reliance. . . . The primary responsibility of developing their economies remains with the African least developed countries themselves and the total political commitment of the Member States to the pursuit of these objectives is necessary . . . [and] social and economic reforms should be undertaken . . . to ensure full participation of the people in the development process. . . . [We] confirm our full adherence to the plan of Action, adopted at the Assembly of Heads of State and Government for implementing the Monrovia Strategy for the Economic, Social and Cultural Development of Africa and to adopting, among other measures, those relating to the setting up of regional structures and strengthening of those already existing for an eventual establishment of an African Economic Community.

And finally "recalling the Monrovia Declaration of Commitment on the guiding principles and steps to be taken to achieve national and collective self-reliant economic and social development for a new international economic order," the resolution, among other things,

1. Adopts the plan of Action for the implementation of the Monrovia Strategy hereafter called the Lagos Plan of Action;
2. Appeals to all Member States to take all necessary measures to implement the Lagos Plan of Action at national, sub-regional and continental levels;
3. Requests all OAU Member States and the African Group at the UN to support this plan.

To attain the objectives, the LPA, among other things, says importance should be accorded to the development of the agricultural base in order to achieve, not only self-sufficiency in food production, but also production of adequate surplus. . . . For the 1980s emphasis should be given to the development of agriculture and agro-based industries . . . co-operation . . . and the satisfaction of basic needs.''

Two other areas of interest emphasized in the document are those of institutions and the difficulties facing them in carrying out their programs. The development of institutions is stressed; they should be of a type that can help their members to develop collectively their capabilities and infrastructures essential for their social and economic development.

The LPA also admitted the difficulties facing African multinational institutions in performing their functions. One major problem identified is their inability to follow up in the implementation of political decisions. There are two reasons: lack of financial and material support, and lack of political support.

At this stage, because institutions are crucial to development, it is worthwhile to make some observations on the problems of African multinational institutions. The main problems are those of number and political support. The LAP advocates the development of institutions by creating more of them and developing and strengthening existing ones. But, at present, what is clear is that already there are more multinational African institutions than the governments can support. Therefore views about reducing their number have been coming from different subregions of the continent.

The other problem is lack of political support to the institutions, which explains the lack of financial and material support they are suffering. Another explanation for poor financial and material endowment might in fact be the great number of the institutions, which tax the resources and patience of member countries in terms of contributions. With this situation, it is obvious that African institutions cannot follow up the implementation of political decisions because of lack of political, financial, and material support. This seems to show that the key lack is political support or will, which leads to the crucial questions: Why lack of political support? Why should African countries be in the paradoxical position of needing and establishing more institutions and yet abandoning them financially and materially after they have been established?

These are very important questions whose answers are elusive but crucial to the clarification of Africa's development problems. The problem of political will has been the greatest stumbling block to Africa's development. Therefore, if the whys and hows of this problem are found, Africa will have gone a long way toward solving its development problems. It is to be hoped that researchers will devote time and resources to these questions.

On the side of speculation, several reasons could be mooted for the lack of political will, the first perhaps being sociopolitical instability. At present there are countries, particularly in Southern Africa, that are still fighting liberation wars. There are also countries fighting civil wars or wars among themselves. This was the case in Uganda until recently and is still the case in Sudan, Chad, Libya, and Ethiopia. And of the remaining African countries, most have one type of instability or another arising from a variety of internal factors such as religion, ethnicity, gaps in income, and access to wealth.

One could also speculate about concern with development issues and power struggles among political factions or interest groups. The latter phenomenon, like the one of political instability, tends to reflect the fragility of African politics. The development factor may not be a good explanation of lack of political will. The assumption is that African governments are too much engrossed with development problems and there is too much to do for them to have time and resources to devote to their multinational organizations. From my experience, I am sceptical about genuine interest of African countries in development. I have worked on development problems for some years now, but I have not seen any evidence of African leaders' genuine commitment to development. If there were any, then they have been hindered by either internal political factors or external factors, or both, but have not made genuine efforts to neutralize such factors. On the contrary, what has been displayed by African leadership is laxity and complacency. If African leaders are little interested in developing their people, then what *have* they been doing, and what *are* they interested in?

This is where the question of the struggle for power comes in. Power confers the capability to deploy resources; it also confers fame, prestige, and privileges. Consequently, those who are in power are loath to relinquish it, while there are those who are ceaselessly struggling to attain it.

And at a slightly lower level, there are those who fight at all costs to maintain the positions they have acquired even if they are not fit for them. They want to do so for the same reasons, namely power, fame, prestige, and privileges. In addition, power confers a good living standard comparable with the industrialized countries. Those in such positions fear to lose their privileges. They also fear having their ego hurt if they lose power. Hence the fierce struggle to defend their positions stoutly against those who are fighting their way up. Perhaps this attitude is explained by poverty and the lack of realization that one can contribute to society in an infinite number of ways. If this is correct, then one supposes that the elimination of poverty will do away with the struggle for privileges, which are at present few. Similarly, if there is a realization that one could contribute to society in different ways without having power and that such a contribution can finally reward one with fame and prestige, then the struggle for power may abate. The example of such contributions have come from dedicated religious and charity workers. Even if they disliked it, the work of such people has always been accompanied by fame and prestige.

I have dwelt long on the LPA because of its importance in pioneering Africa's serious thinking on economic problems. Several other resolutions followed the LPA, for example, the Harare Declaration, which was a product of the Thirteenth FAO Regional Conference for Africa held July 16–25, 1984 in Harare, Zimbabwe. Africa's ministers of agriculture and livestock and rural development assembled and made a declaration on Africa's economic problems and their intention to tackle them resolutely. I will examine what I consider to be the salient aspects of the declaration.

The Harare Declaration stressed four areas of effort: self-reliance, food and agricultural production, food security, and the focus on Africa by the FAO and other organizations. I will discuss the questions of self-reliance, the role of the FAO and other organizations, and the conclusion of the declaration.

With respect to self-reliance, the declaration had this to say:

We affirm our determination to become controllers of our destinies and to this end we assert our rightful role both at the national and international level. We solemnly renew our commitment to the establishment of a New International Economic Order through the implementation of goals and objectives of the International Development Strategy for the Third Development Decade, the Regional Food Plan for Africa (AFPLAN), the Lagos Plan of Action, the Declaration of Principles and Programme of Action of the World Conference on Agrarian Reform and Rural Development, the new concept for the implementation of the Plan of Action on World Food Security, and the Strategy for Fisheries Management and Development.

On the role of the FAO and other organizations in focusing on Africa, the document says, "We call on all international organizations and donor agencies to increase their financial and material assistance to accelerate agricultural development in the Region."

The Declaration concludes "We solemnly put forth this Harare Declaration on the food crisis in Africa in conviction that we possess the will and capacity and have the full support of the international community to feed all our peoples and to lay the foundation for greater economic prosperity and self-reliance in Africa."

There are two things to note about the above quotations: self-reliance versus external assistance; and the will and the capacity to feed their peoples and lay the foundation for greater economic prosperity and self-reliance.

The question of self-reliance has been echoed many times in different forums. But it is noteworthy that any declaration of self-reliance is usually accompanied by solicitation of assistance from the international community. If both aspects of self-reliance and assistance from donors are stressed equally, then there is a conflict. One only hopes that self-reliance is stressed far more than assistance from outside: no self-reliance is feasible while Africa is always looking to the outside world for help. The recent trend, even in multilateral organizations, should awaken Africa. Contributions to these institutions are being cut and hence aid resources are becoming scarcer than ever before. Donors are also cutting back their direct contributions to Africa and are beginning to lose interest. I will develop these arguments further in chapter 6.

For self-reliance to come about, both the will and the capacity for development must be present. Capacity exists in terms of resources, but it needs to be activated by the will, and it is this that is lacking. Otherwise, the capacity would have been applied. What happens is that the will is directed outward toward aid which, it is thought, will accelerate development. Aid might help, but that depends on the type as well as utilization by the recipient. However, one thing should be clear: there is no free aid, no matter how one thinks about it. This argument will also be developed in chapter 6.

Groping for solutions to Africa's crisis continued, this time at the level of the OAU. As I indicated earlier, that organization has now shifted emphasis from political to economic matters, and its recent meetings have reflected this. One such meeting was the one held by planning and economic ministers in February 1985 in preparation for the summit of Africa's heads of state and government. Fifty countries attended, a reflection of the meeting's importance. It recommended well-formulated development strategies and plans for Africa's development and advised that governments should gradually increase the share of agriculture in total national public investment to between 20 and 25 percent by 1989. The heads of state and government met July 18–20, 1985 and endorsed these recommendations, thus transforming them into declarations and resolutions. This looks like a serious undertaking, but it will be at least another five years before an assessment can be made. However, at present there seems to be more ground for doubt than for optimism. This is reflected in the outward-looking strategy for solving Africa's development problems.

EXTERNAL SOLUTIONS

I am not advocating a clear-cut division between internal and external solutions. Some of these, proposed as internal solutions, are very much outward-looking. However, in terms of internal solutions, much of the thinking seems to have been generated internally, or, if externally, say by the FAO, Africans commanded the deliberations. In the case of external solutions, I want to identify these with Africa's participation in UN organizations and the Program for the Economic Recovery of Africa (PERA).

However, before discussing Africa's participation in UN organizations, it is necessary to add a caveat, for two reasons. First, Africa is a member of so many of these organizations that the subject of its relations with them is of a very large scope and complicated nature. Hence, the subject would require a separate study that is beyond the scope of the present one. But this is an important area of investigation that I hope other scholars will examine in detail.

The international community has channeled a substantial amount of resources to Africa through the UN agencies. It would therefore be useful for policy as well as interesting to know what these resources were, the forms they took, the sectors of the economy they were directed to, and the way in which they have been managed.

Second, my view is that Africa's development problems and their proposed solutions are well known. They have been talked about in several forums and analyzed and documented in various forms. This is the case especially with externally derived and oriented ideas about development problems and their solutions, many of which came from the UN agencies. Therefore there is no need to repeat these ideas in detail here. Hence only a few UN agencies are mentioned in connection with Africa's relations with them, and this at a very general level.

African countries have been members of many international organizations. Therefore, over the years, they have been partners to various declarations and resolutions and have committed themselves to many plans and UN decades of action. Some of these have been mentioned in the previous section. However, a few more examples of organizations in which African countries are members need to be added, for it is from them that Africa seeks external solutions to its problems. One such organization is, of course, the United Nations. However, it is its specialized agencies that are more relevant to Africa for the purpose of social and economic development. Examples of these are UNCTAD, the World Health Organization, the International Labor Organization, the United Nations Environmental Program, the United Nations Educational, Scientific, and Cultural Organization, the United Nations Children's Fund, UNIDO, to list a few major ones. The FAO, which is a very important organization for Africa, has already been mentioned above in relation to its role in the Harare Declaration. Some of the plans to which Africa committed itself through these and many other organizations are the United Nations Plan of Action to Combat Desertification (1977), the World Conservation Strategy (1981), and the International Agreement on Tropical Timber. Africa is also a member of the World Food Program. The expectation, of course, is that the international community will channel resources through these multinational organizations to Africa. However, the issue here is not whether these resources have been forthcoming or not; it is the extent to which Africa is relying on the international community to resolve its internal development contradictions. The degree of dependence on, and the expectations from, the international community are too high; my argument is that as a result there can be no development whatsoever, no matter how long Africa waits.

There are two other UN institutions with which Africa is closely associated that merit discussion with respect to Africa's externally derived development solutions. These are the Economic Commission for Africa (ECA) and the IBRD.

The latter has already been discussed in chapter 3 in a different context. Here it merits discussion in relation to the agenda for action that it recommended to Africa as a solution to its development crisis.

The ECA is located in Africa and designed to help sort out its development problems and tackle them. There are similar institutions for Latin America and Asia. The ECA has long been an adviser to African countries on development problems. In the context of this discussion, its special memorandum on Africa's socioeconomic problems are relevant.

It is common knowledge that the ECA, since its establishment, has produced a huge quantity of documents and is still preoccupied with that function. Most, if not all, of these documents are meant to provide information as well as advice to African countries on their development problems. But recently the ECA produced a document of special interest to Africa titled "ECA Special Memorandum." What makes it special is perhaps the timing: it came out at the time of Africa's economic crisis, when the continent is frantically groping for solutions. The situation is so pressing that quick and special solutions are needed. In particular, the memorandum demands quick action by the policy makers. Briefly, some of its recommendations are:

1. the urgent design of strategy effectively to counter natural disasters;
2. the designation of agricultural and manpower development as urgent priorities;
3. research, development, and dissemination of technologies;
4. the development of social and physical infrastructures to enhance agricultural production; and
5. interregional and intra-African cooperation.

In sum, the emphasis is on agricultural production.

Similarly, the World Bank has by now issued tremendous quantities of documents on Third World economic problems and their solutions. This accumulation of information is continuing and will continue for as long as the IBRD remains relevant to capitalist economic problems. In the same vein, the World Bank, like many other UN agencies, has over the years been analyzing Africa's development problems and proposing solutions. And like the ECA, the World Bank, in 1981, came up with a document titled "Accelerated Development in Sub-Saharan Africa: An Agenda for Action." Also, the bank has recently been promoting the Special Facility for Africa and expects to raise $2 billion.

The document is a response to the continually worsening economic situation of Africa in the years that preceded it. In fact, since its publication the situation has further deteriorated. "An Agenda for Action" is intended as a blueprint for the solution of the continent's development problems and covers a wide range of topics. However, it concluded that obstacles "can only be surmounted by the joint efforts of African governments and the donor community." And increased aid and technical assistance "can only be mobilized if they support deliberate and well formulated programmes to reverse the downward trend of development in Africa." This, according to the agenda, entails "technically difficult and politically thorny" policy reforms. In a nutshell, the document calls for more efficient use of resources as well as political will.

In addition to the points discussed above, one area of special interest, agriculture and rural development, is of special interest because it is at the root of Africa's current development crisis. In this regard, the agenda stressed the following areas for attention: (1) a focus on smallholder production; (2) a change in the incentive structure by increasing producer prices, developing a more open and competitive marketing arrangement, and involving farmers in the decisions that affect them; (3) the expansion of agricultural research; (4) the implementation of quick-yielding activities in agriculture, and (5) the rehabilitation of existing schemes.

Insofar as the agricultural and rural development element of development strategy is concerned, the ECA special memorandum and the IBRD's agenda for action have a lot or almost everything in common. This is especially true with respect to research, pricing and marketing policies, provision of appropriate physical infrastructures, and rehabilitation of existing schemes. And these are things that have been known for a long time. The same ideas and information have been circulated between agencies for years—and UN agencies have been one another's sources of reference or information in their reports or documents.

As I indicated earlier, Africa's participation in UN agencies is only one of the two major sources of external solutions to PERA. However, PERA is fundamentally different from other externally derived solutions. In the case of others, the solutions take the form of ideas, proposals, or blueprints for strategies. In the case of PERA, the solution is expected to take the form of financial assistance. In this respect, the program is estimated to cost $128 billion with an anticipated $48 billion from external sources. This is foreign aid, and it appears more appropriate to discuss it in chapter 6. However, it is mentioned here because it is considered by Africa as some sort of special solution born of its difficult and special economic circumstances. PERA carries an aura of seriousness on the part of Africa to solve its economic problems; unlike previous proposals, this one was debated and endorsed by the UN General Assembly. Yet it seems to be faltering just one year after its formulation. At the meeting of the OAU Council of Ministers that was held from Febuary 23–28, 1987, the secretary general of the organization revealed that Africa's economic recovery program is stalled because the international community has not responded as expected. OAU sources are quoted as saying that "there is as yet little or no evidence of concerted international measures backing the programme one year after it was launched." This observation, though admittedly after a very short period, should be a warning to Africa.

If Africa has not learned the lesson that externally derived and oriented solutions are no solutions and only encourage dependence, then it should learn it now. African leaders should long ago have grasped that the onus for developing Africa rests squarely on Africans themselves and that the starting point is unity.

However, the sources of the solutions notwithstanding, all the solutions have failed, for reasons that will be further examined in the remaining chapters.

5 Rural Development: A Viable Alternative Strategy?

During this period enough studies have been done, sufficient experience gained, more than adequate research and observations have been made to validate certain assumptions and to provide insight into the basic and fundamental requirements for successful planning operation and functioning of rural development programmes.

Iraj Poostchi

We must study the farmer not patronize him: we must assume that he knows his business better than we do, unless there is evidence to the contrary.

Polly Hill

In the first four chapters of this book, I discussed the development models, the global and African setting of the prevailing crisis, and the solutions being tried by African countries. Twenty-five years of application of past development models have failed to develop Africa. In the course of application, the models underwent some modifications with notions like "growth with distribution" and the "basic needs approach," but still they failed.

As I indicated in chapters 2 and 3, the failure of these models has been associated with external and internal factors, especially the former. It is only recently that African countries started admitting that they are also substantially responsible for the crisis. My argument, in fact, is that they are far more responsible than any exogenous factors because they left their economies too open, which logically led them to espouse development strategies that are outward-looking. There is hardly a single African country south of the Sahara that fashioned a people-centered development policy, hence the failure of a development strategy that not only is not people-centered but also derived its inspiration from externally constructed development models.

The groping for solutions continued at the level of both the OAU and the UN agencies, but still there is no sign of a solution to the predicament. The question then is: What next? The answer is: Rural development. It is the only viable alternative strategy. In this chapter, three major areas will be discussed, namely the nature of rural development, the relationship between it and self-reliance, and the problems of rural development.

WHAT IS RURAL DEVELOPMENT?

In order for rural development to be a success, there should be a clear and generally accepted definition of it. But alas there is none. People tend to associate rural development vaguely with activities in rural areas designed to improve living conditions with a view to stemming rural-urban migration. This view is a selfish one, and yet it prevailed for many years until the recent signs of reorientation. It is selfish in the sense that the purpose is to enhance urban life. Too many people in the urban areas would crowd the cities, stretch social services, increase filth, and raise the level of crime, with the obvious effect of a lower standard of living for urban dwellers. Yet the relatively high standard of urban life is made possible by resources from the rural areas, which subsidize the urban ones. This is selfish, and it is a misguided development strategy.

However, it is now encouraging to note that in recent years, people have started to think in terms of sympathy toward the rural populace and the enhancement of its productive capacity. Despite this positive development, there is still a long way to go in terms not only of positive impact on rural life but, perhaps even more important, also of a clear understanding of what rural development is. Nonetheless, efforts are continuing toward a clear and generally accepted definition. Advanced thinking is even moving toward the articulation of a theory of rural development. Meantime, let us look at some of the efforts that have been made toward a definition.

Governments and donor agencies engage in rural activities designed to improve rural life, the former mainly through their field administrations and the latter through their field representatives working with government representatives and the people themselves. Looking at rural development in this way, then, one could give a prominent place to local governments, which are nearer to the people and provide them with services. This perception of rural development, namely provision of services through institutions, has led some governments and donor agencies to define rural development organizationally, that is, as the provision of services coordinated by more than one government agency.

Another school of thought defines rural development in terms of several elements such as: (1) disparate activities in a given area; (2) self-sustaining productive and income-generating activities; (3) subsidized delivery of economic and social services; and (4) local organizations engaged in developmental activities, or what is otherwise known as people's participation (Guidelines 1984).

The FAO approached the definition of rural development in another way: through defining projects. Surely, definition of rural development projects is not synonymous with a definition of rural development: the latter is a broader concept under which the former is subsumed. Yet there are two advantages in defining a rural development project: first, it is a step toward the definition of rural development, and second, it helps sharpen such a definition.

But before the definition propounded by the FAO is examined, some observations with respect to the broad categorization of rural development projects are necessary. Rural development projects may be defined according to their types and their aims. One may distinguish two types at the general level: the directly productive and income-generating projects and those intended to provide social services and infrastructures. Projects that are productive and income-generating could, for example, be formulated in the fields of agriculture, livestock, fishery, forestry, poultry, and cottage industries. Examples of projects that provide social services and infrastructures are those concerned with water supply, health, education, electricity, roads, markets, and motor parks for commercial vehicles.

The aims of rural development projects have been well articulated by the FAO. There are three major aims, namely: (1) to improve directly or indirectly the capabilities and well-being of rural people; (2) to facilitate the participation of the rural poor in project identification, implementation, and decision making; and (3) to help the rural poor in different environments solve their own problems.

Whichever way one defines it, the history of rural development tends to show a shift of emphasis from provision of services only to the encouragement of productive activities. The former agrees with the definition held by some governments and donor agencies mentioned above. Governments and their field administrations and local authorities perceived rural development as provision of services and inputs and technical advice to the rural people. But in recent years the economic problems of Africa have forced a shift in emphasis toward the mobilization of local resources for productive activities. In this shift, rural development was now perceived as people's participation and capacity building, and new concepts such as self-help, self-reliance, people's participation, and nongovernmental organizations (NGOs) gained prominence. People's participation and the role of the NGOs have commanded particular attention because both have a political dimension. Governments may be wary about the effects on the populace of the activities of the NGOs. Fears are expressed that some NGOs may deliberately try to enlighten the people about their rights vis-à-vis the government. Other NGOs may limit themselves to their work, but in the course of it the rural poor may find out on their own about their rights and potential power. In both cases, once the rural poor build their productive capacity and perceive their potential power, they may pose a threat to the established power structures. Hence the apprehension of not only the constituted authorities but also the rural power elite.

People are empowered in two ways, through participation in decision making and productive activities and through the enhancement of their productive power. This means that participation has both political and economic dimensions—there seems to be no sharp distinction between the two. But one thing is clear: they reinforce each other. Political participation, through facilitating access to decision making, facilitates access to economic resources. Similarly, the building of productive capacity enhances economic power and hence access to political resources in terms of the creation of new and the enhancement of existing institutions through which participation in decision making is facilitated.

People's participation entails the mobilization of people through associations and organizations to share in economic and political power and the benefits of economic growth. The access to economic assets and political power poses a threat to entrenched local interests, both governmental and nongovernmental. It requires great courage and sacrifice on the part of both the government and local elites to accede to sharing power, assets, and the benefits of economic growth with the rural poor. And in fact this is the most difficult and delicate problem of rural development once a clear definition has been developed. The conventional wisdom maintains that the major problems of rural development are lack of economic resources and institutional capability. This is true, but relatively easier to resolve. Resources are always scarce, no matter how physically abundant, in the sense that they are exhaustible and therefore they have to be used economically. If resources were available in inexhaustible supply, there would be no need for the science of economics. Yet, relative to the rural needs, I maintain that resources are not a serious constraint. The problem is that of lack of access to them on the part of rural people, for obvious reasons.

The lack of institutional capability is more important as a constraint than economic resources. Yet this problem is also relatively easier to solve than that constituted by the local power elite. The latter problem is the most delicate one in the design of rural development programs and projects. Resources are available, and, with concerted effort and concentration of resources, institutional capability could be built over time, but still the local power structures might continue to be a great hindrance to the realization of rural development objectives. Many governments may be keenly interested in uplifting the living standard of their rural populace, but in the effort to do so they may face stiff, if subtle, opposition from the local power structure. Therefore the crux of the matter is how to break this power. One answer is obviously to organize people to enhance their access to political and economic resources. But this is easier said than done. There are two major stumbling blocks. One is the capacity of the local power elite to sabotage any effort in organizing the local population, possibly by using their economic and political clout to blackmail the populace. This means that it requires great courage, sacrifice, and perseverance to succeed. And these are the most difficult attributes to find in a poor community.

The other obstacle to organizing the people is the relationship of the local power structure with the government. This is what I mean by their political power. Their political power resides in their relations with politicians and bureaucrats. And at the bottom of this is their economic power: they are of help to politicians by both their economic power and their local influence. They can make or unmake a politician; they can help win or lose elections; and so, in this way, the politician is dependent on them. Their power over bureaucrats is a matter of outright graft. In this respect, both have a corrupt symbiotic relationship. The bureaucrats obtain money or some material benefit or influence from the local power structure. The latter is, in turn, rewarded with easy access to government services such as agricultural inputs, commercial services, and credit. With this political and bureaucratic backing, the local power elite can easily subvert any attempt at people's organization. Therefore, for the rural populace, the struggle is going to be a long and painful one. For them the paradox is this: they have power and yet they do not have it. They have power when they organize, yet they are very weak relative to their antagonists, namely the local power structure. The people lack economic resources and access to them.

We have come a long way in the effort to define rural development. I have shown that it is perceived in terms of three things: (1) the organization and coordination of the provision of services; (2) the objectives of rural development projects; and (3) people's participation and capacity building. Yet discussions of the definition of rural development will be incomplete without reference to the notion of integration. In recent years there has been some movement from the notion of rural development to that of "integrated rural development." What is the latter? My understanding is that this concept means the interconnecting of all activities concerned with rural programs in a given area.

As I pointed out earlier, there are two broad aspects of rural development, one dealing with social services and infrastructures and the other with productive and income-generating activities. Both aspects entail activities at the project level that may be disparate or constituted into separate programs. When these are fashioned into a single program in such a way as to complement one another, the result is an integrated rural development program. Such programs are designed so that no sector of the rural economy is left out or neglected. None of the sectors should lag behind or its growth be adversely affected by faster growth in another sector or sectors. In addition, activities in all sectors are simultaneously pursued. In short, programs and projects should meet the conditions of interwoveness, complementarity, and simultaneity of implementation and progress.

There is hope that one day a theory of rural development will be constructed. Surely, there is need for one, for it would enhance clarity in the formulation and implementation of programs and projects. So, efforts at a clear definition will contribute immensely to the construction of a rural development theory. But though the theory is necessary, it is impossible to wait for it. In this respect practice must inspire theory. This is the reverse of what happens in Africa, where theory has always inspired practice. It is one of the most serious problems of the continent. In addition, the theories have so far been exogenous, rooted outside African society and experience. This is one of the main explanations of the multiplicity of failures. Therefore one condition for Africa's success is that practice must inspire theory, which must derive endogenously from African experience and social conditions.

WHY RURAL DEVELOPMENT?

This question has been partially answered in the opening of this chapter. Past development models and their modifications failed. African countries groped for solutions and settled on rural development as an alternative model. For most countries, it is a relatively new alternative; at least, it has not been taken seriously until recently. At the time the strategy was adopted, it was merely perceived as a way of providing social services and infrastructures to the rural areas, not for any productive purpose but as a bait to retain the people in the countryside. The idea was that improvement in rural life would persuade the people to stay, thus eliminating the menace of rural-urban migration, which makes life in the cities intolerable. In this respect the strategy failed because it was faulty from the beginning. Neither was it based on the improvement of the productive capacity of the rural areas nor did it encourage people's participation. Governments thought they knew the needs of the people in the rural areas and embarked on providing for them. However, whether these needs were perceived correctly or not, the problem is that governments could not continue to provide the services in adequate quantities and quality. Hence the need for some contribution from the people themselves, which is reflected in the current shift of emphasis to the productive and participatory aspect of rural development. Whether the new emphasis will succeed or not is a moot question, for it is still too early to judge. But indications from some studies point toward optimism.

The other reason for choosing rural development as an alternative is its connection with self-reliance. Ever since the intensification of Africa's socioeconomic crisis, self-reliance has become more important than ever before, a reflection of the realization that African economies have depended too much on external factors, which have been responsible for much of the decline of these economies. The economies swung with the fortunes of the industrialized world. Therefore self-reliance is perceived as the only way to shield African economies against these violent oscillations. Surely, this is the best alternative, but again it is easier said than done. I have pointed out in chapter 4 the contradiction between the principle of self-reliance and the practice of heavy reliance on the international community for aid. In this respect, then, is self-reliance just more rhetoric? There are indications that it is, for example, in the amount of resources deployed to agriculture and rural development by African governments. There is a huge gap between the noise made about self-reliance and the resources deployed to bring it about. The allocation of 20–25 percent of public resources to agriculture by 1989 does not address the problem at all because the amount is meager. It is a case of 20–25 percent of resources allocated to 75–80 percent of the population. There is no way such a tiny amount of resources could have a positive impact on such a large proportion of the population, which is growing rapidly and unabatedly. For this reason I am firmly convinced that, in reality, the principle of self-reliance, insofar as African countries are concerned, is still very much on the level of rhetoric.

African countries may adopt the strategy of self-reliance seriously or complacently. But one fact remains: its adoption is eminently sensible. The question then is: Why? There are two major reasons. One, which has been discussed above, is to insulate African economies against the vagaries of global economic changes. The other reason lies in the fact that abundant resources are available for the liberation of African economies. Africa's most valuable resource is human. There is a great reservoir in the rural areas, perhaps not trained in the elitist sense, but trainable. And what it needs is not elitist training but functional training. In the course of this training, there is also a lot that can be learned from the rural populace. The results of this learning could serve two major purposes. One is the articulation of correct policies, programs, and projects that have a very high probability of succeeding. The other is that the results will help immensely in the construction of rural development theory. This is the case of practice inspiring theory referred to earlier.

Material resources, of which I have already given some examples in chapter 2, are abundant in Africa's rural setting. But the fact is that they are too many to enumerate exhaustively. The forests alone are a source of a great number of resources.

Thus Africa does not require external resources except training in science, technology, and research. Even this is necessary only within a given period of time, after which Africa should be able to modify and replicate the training according to its needs deriving from its experience and socioeconomic circumstances.

With this huge resource base, Africa should not be dependent at all. Therefore the perpetuation of existing dependency cannot be excused. The need for change is obvious and overdue, and the principle of self-reliance provides a good guide. One of its great merits is that it makes development people-centered; and this is the only strategy that could pull Africa out of its present socioeconomic crisis. A people-centered development strategy will tap dormant resources, thus facilitating endogenous solutions.

Much of rural development is synonymous with agriculture and allied facets such as livestock, fisheries, and forestry. Even cottage industries must depend almost wholly on agricultural activities. In this sense, agriculture is the bedrock of any economy. In Africa, agriculture and related activities employ no less than 70 percent of the population. So the crucial importance of agriculture is very clear.

In addition, let us look at other dimensions of the importance of agriculture in a national economy. Two basic ones are the food supply and raw materials. Food is a basic need: it sustains life and provides energy for further production—to the urban industrial worker, the bureaucrat, the manager, and the politician. It does the same for the rural populace. Agriculture also provides raw materials for industrial production, both for cottage industries in the rural areas and for major industries in the urban areas. It is common knowledge that goods and services spewed from the industrial system, whether urban or rural, meet our daily needs.

Let me further underscore the importance briefly. Agriculture is a great industry in the West, where its importance is reflected in several fundamental ways. First, it provides a proportion of the raw materials needed by Western industries. Second, agricultural products provide sensitive trading commodities among the Western nations. This sensitivity is illustrated not only by the losses that an agricultural trade war between Western nations occasions but also by the intensity of the conflict. For an example, in 1971 it was estimated that the United States lost $2.5 billion in terms of welfare when it imposed tariffs and quotas on European products. There are many other examples. And such losses, whether in welfare or revenue, are not limited to the United States. Europe has experienced the same whenever there were trade restrictions between the two continents or among the European nations themselves. As to the intensification of conflict between Europe and the United States in agricultural trade, again history is clear: from 1959 to date, Europe and the United States have occasionally been locked in trade conflicts over both agricultural and industrial commodities.

At the country level let us take the United Kingdom as a further illustration of the importance of agriculture to a national economy. For a long time, the United Kingdom was dependent upon imports for its food and raw materials and at one time was the largest importer of agricultural products in the world. But with changing global conditions, especially the collapse of the empire and the rise of competitors, the United Kingdom realized its precarious dependence on such critical agricultural commodities. So, in response, in 1968 it set specific goals for import substitution in agricultural products. And as a consequence, a few years later, domestic production provided some 70 percent of total consumption of temperate zone agricultural products.

The industrialized nations have long realized the importance of food and agriculture as a strategic and sensitive matter. Food was considered the ultimate strategic good and its price a politically sensitive matter. So policies were formulated and implemented to ensure minimum food security by adopting the strategy of import substitution to ensure food self-sufficiency. Perhaps the best way to stress the importance of agriculture in the industrial economies of the West is to quote a passage that speaks for itself.

In essentially all countries the agricultural industry is supported, planned, and managed to a degree which is without parallel in any other sector of the economy with the possible exception of defence industries.In many countries agriculture is managed almost as a public utility, with government planning the level and composition of output, ensuring the availability of inputs, regulating the prices of both, and guaranteeing the return to resources engaged in the industry. (T. K. Warley in Shonfield)

With such importance given to agriculture, it is not surprising that European and American governments consistently subordinate efficiency to economic and social concerns in agricultural policy. In so doing, they consistently and unanimously reject the market model for agriculture. Agricultural policymakers correctly perceived that national economic and political sovereignty, the ability to achieve important social goals, and the capability to protect the national economy from external instabilities all vary inversely with the degree of dependence on the world economy. Additionally, even in industrialized countries, agriculture is still used as an instrument of rural development, or at least in solving rural problems.

The prominence given to agriculture by even the strongest nations in the world offers much food for thought to African countries. They should pay close attention to: (1) the change of policy by the United Kingdom toward self-reliance in agricultural products by applying the strategy of import substitution; (2) the recognition of food as a strategic and sensitive commodity; and (3) the recognition that only an economy with a firm agricultural base can even partially successfully insulate itself from the instabilities of the world economy. It is these penetrating recognitions that have convinced the industrialized nations to throw the market model to the winds and subordinate efficiency to economic and social concerns in agricultural policies. The lessons for Africa are clear. Either it learns these lessons and summons the political will to apply them, or the continent will sink in the turbulent water of rhetoric. There is no alternative.

There is still one important question to ask, namely: Is rural development the sole viable strategy? It appears that it is indeed viable, but can it go it alone? What, for instance, should be the role of industry? How should it complement rural development? Discussions hardly mention industry even if it is of the cottage type, which is easily associable with rural development programs. Perhaps two reasons explain this tendency. The first is the criticism of the policy of industrialization that African countries initially embarked upon immediately after attaining political independence. The second is the perception of industry as solely an urban affair. Let us examine the two.

I am one of the critics of heavy reliance on industrialization as a strategy for development at the expense of a strong agricultural base to sustain the industry, for two reasons. First, African economies are subsistence economies heavily dependent on agriculture and employing well over 80 percent of the population one and a half decades ago. Second, no industry can survive without an uninterrupted supply of food and raw materials from agriculture. For this reason, any industry based on a weak agricultural base will collapse because it will be dependent on external sources not only for capital goods and spare parts but also for raw materials that could be produced easily internally. African countries have since discovered these problems. Almost all their import substitution industries either are shut down or operate well below capacity for lack of, among other things, raw materials. Good examples of this predicament are Nigeria and Tanzania, where industrial production has sunk to 20–40 percent of capacity. Yet, these deficiencies notwithstanding, I am not suggesting that industrialization should be abandoned. It should rather be rationalized. As a start, few critical areas should be selected for concentration of resources and development. Critical industries should be ones that will directly extend production, thereby building the productive capacity of the economy.

The perception of industry as being exclusively urban is also partly responsible for the fact that industry is seldom mentioned in relation to rural development. But what of cottage industry, which is mainly rural-based? The connection between agriculture and cottage industry should be so obvious as to generate lively and serious discussion, but it does not seem to. Even when integrated rural development is talked of, the central role of the word *integrated* is ignored, and hence no one thinks about integrating productive, service, and infrastructure activities to rural industries. Where policies and programs of rural industries do exist, they function on their own, completely independent of any integration. This leaves much out of the integrative element of rural development.

The link between urban industries and agriculture is obvious. Apart from providing food and raw materials, agriculture could also provide people. In the first instance, agricultural development may provide surplus raw materials that the urban industries may not be able to absorb, but there are two alternative solutions: to expand industry to absorb the surplus or to sell the surplus. The former solution is of course superior and the one at which African countries should aim. The latter should be avoided, for it is the one that perpetuates dependency and subjects African economies to violent instabilities.

Similarly, the rise of agricultural productivity in rural areas will make people available for urban employment after the needs of the cottage industries and other services have been satisfied. This movement of people further underscores the importance of rational linking of rural development programs with industrialization.

So, in sum, rural development is a genuine alternative development model, but care should be taken that it does not underemphasize the importance of industrialization in a few critical areas, for a start. Rural development strategy should be designed in such a way as to accommodate the needs of industrialization. The two should be harmonized, integrated.

PROBLEMS OF RURAL DEVELOPMENT

Sub-Saharan Africa has accepted rural development as an alternative strategy for development, but we have seen that there is no clearly articulated and generally accepted definition of the term. And a theory of rural development is still far away, though efforts may be underway in different places to construct one. However, the problems are not limited to lack of proper definition and lack of theory. There are many others of a practical type.

Lack of proper definition and theory notwithstanding, rural development has been practiced for some years in different ways in different countries. The variations are explained by factors such as political and institutional structures, soioeconomic conditions, and historical experience. There are also similarities due to the common problems posed by Africa's socioeconomic conditions. But whatever the differences or similarities, one thing is clear: that rural development, in some form, somehow, has been practiced by countries for some time now, and experience has been gained therefrom.

The questions then are: What is this experience? And does it indicate any hope for rural development as a viable development strategy for Africa? The attempt to find answers to these questions might throw some light on the search for a clear definition of rural development.

But before any detailed discussion of the problems of rural development, it seems worthwhile to present a few examples of the general socioeconomic conditions in some countries. The first consideration is the size of the population that is rural or occupied in agriculture. In Botswana 84 percent of the population is rural or agricultural; in Malawi, 90 percent; in Uganda, 88 percent; in Tanzania, 94 percent; Burkina Faso, 90 percent; and Sierra Leone, over 90 percent; Sudan, 80 percent; Mozambique, 84 percent; Senegal, 70 percent; Zimbabwe, 75 percent; Swaziland, 85 percent; Zambia, 60 percent; and Congo, 50 percent.

Another important general factor is the availability of arable land. For example: Botswana has 7 percent; Lesotho, 12 percent, with a serious problem of erosion arising from steep terrain and overgrazing. In Tanzania, 50–60 percent of the land is arable, and only 15.7 percent of that is under cultivation; in Uganda, 40 percent of arable land is utilized; in Nigeria only 5.5m hectares, representing 34.4 percent of tillable land, are under cultivation; in Sierra Leone there are 5m hectares of arable land, but only about 800,000 hectares, or 8 percent is cultivated. Zimbabwe is an interesting case: 60 percent of its land is suitable for raising livestock. But it has a colonial settlement problem: 6,000 European farmers held 51 percent of the available land, while 700,000 African families engage in subsistence production; but the European sector commands 90 percent of total sales of agricultural products.

Production is also an important aspect of agriculture. Again only a few examples will be given here. In Mozambique agriculture contributes 40 percent to GDP and accounts for 80 percent of exports; in Swaziland, 31 percent of GDP and 70 percent of exports; in Senegal, 30 percent of GDP; Burkina Faso, 45 percent of GDP. In Nigeria agriculture provided 20 percent of GDP in 1974 and decreased to 18 percent in 1981, and its contribution to exports followed a similar trend, with 32 percent in 1970 and 5 percent in 1980. A country similar to Nigeria in this respect is Congo, where agriculture accounts for only 6.8 percent of the GDP. This is not surprising because both countries are oil economies where the tendency to neglect agriculture has always been strong. Meanwhile Sudan, like Ghana with cocoa, seems to provide a good example of monocultural economy, with cotton accounting for 60 percent of foreign exchange. In Uganda, agriculture provides 50 percent of the GDP and 40 percent of exports. But in recent years the decline in production has been tremendous. On average, most agricultural commodities declined by -64.3 percent. This is not surprising given the instability in the country, which has lasted for many years. There is reason to expect a similar, even if less acute, trend in countries having serious political instability.

The three general factors discussed above are of course not exhaustive. Other aspects such as health, literacy, population growth, nutrition, and mortality have been discussed in chapter 3. Admittedly, the examples of population size, availability of arable land, and agricultural production came from a few countries, but there is evidence to show that they represent the general trend in Africa. Recent estimates are that 75–80 percent of the population live in the rural areas. Africa does not yet have a single industrialized country. Therefore the base of African economies is agriculture. And potentials in agriculture are still great. Only 26 percent of arable land in Africa is under cultivation, and irrigation claimed only a meager 2 percent of the cultivated land in 1975. In sum, the main aim of discussing the three factors above is to emphasize the close link between agriculture and rural development. Though agriculture is not completely synonymous with rural development, the two are inseparable. Hence the need for the high integration of agricultural and rural development policies.

Another very important aspect of rural development is institutional arrangements, the structures through which programs and projects are implemented. I realize that there are a variety of structures in Africa, depending on countries, but in a work of this nature, it is not possible to cover all countries. However, examples from a few nations may reveal institutional similarities and differences between them. The four examples discussed here are Botswana and Malawi in Southern Africa, Kenya in East Africa, and Sierra Leone in West Africa.

In Botswana, an accelerated rural development program was started in 1973. There were four sub–programs, which concentrated on the provision of services and infrastructure. However, in recent years, there has been a shift to productive and employment-generation activities. But of major interest here is the institutional structure used to implement the programs. Available information indicates that district development planning committees were used, which, in turn, worked through village development committees. Each type of committee held a meeting for a few days with the rural people, and it was in this way that the populace was heard. The village committee is usually chaired by the village headman, an example of the use of traditional institutions in development.

Malawi, my second example, had three major rural development programs covering the country. Subsumed under these programs are ten rural growth centres. There is also a rural water supply scheme incorporating many projects. Here again, people's participation is ensured through district development committees, area action groups, and community development activities. District development committees are similar in structure to those in Botswana, but the emphasis in Malawi is on the provision of services and infrastructure.

In Kenya, my third example, the trend is similar. As far back as in 1969, Kenya set up a national rural development committee. This was followed by decentralization of development activities to the provincial and district levels, which provided for divisional and district development committees. Subsequently, in the 1974–78 development plan, the district development committees and district development officers received greater attention. The emphasis increased as time went on, and in the 1984–88 development plan, the "District Development Focus" became the centerpiece of Kenya's development strategy. Here again, the similarity in approach at the district level among Kenya, Botswana, and Malawi should be noted. Another area of similarity is the emphasis on the provision of services and infrastructure such as water and water catchment, small dams, soil conservation, feeder roads, bridges, and so on. Kenya lays great stress on rural roads and to this end has two major programs, one for rural access roads and one for minor roads.

My fourth example, Sierra Leone, has a structure similar to that of Zambia. Sierra Leone has integrated agricultural development programs whereas Zambia has integrated rural development projects but based on the provinces as units of activity. The Sierra Leone programs emphasize extension, processing of agricultural crops, and infrastructure. However, the Rural Development Section of the Ministry of Social Welfare undertakes income-generating activities in addition to infrastructure, literacy, health, nutrition, and appropriate technology. Literacy projects are important because at least 90 percent of the rural population is illiterate, and this is a major handicap to development.

But one other major development problem in Sierra Leone is that of coordination. Like Botswana and Malawi, and indeed many other African countries, Sierra Leone has a firmly rooted traditional institution, but it is not well-utilized, because the chiefs' councils do not coordinate their activities with the government's functional field agencies. This problem of lack of coordination led to the creation of planning units in the provinces and of provincial and district planning committees. At the provincial level there is a similarity with Kenya, and at the district level there is similarity with Botswana and Malawi. But unlike the latter two countries, Sierra Leone does not seem to make good use of its traditional institutions in its development programs.

With the few examples given above, it is now appropriate to discuss the major problems of rural development. The first that spring to mind are administrative ones: those of consultation, coordination, and maintenance and sustenance of projects. Consultation, which is a step toward people's participation, enhances a project's chances of success. Where it is lacking, the obvious result is failure. Coordination problems are brought about by proliferation of institutions as well as the presence of different levels of authority in a given unit. Lack of coordination brings about duplication and waste of time and other resources. Yet it is difficult to solve coordination problems. Much depends on the unit chosen to be the coordinator: because power comes with this role, care should be taken in choosing or creating the coordinating institution.

Maintenance and sustenance of projects are related. To sustain a project, commitment is needed either from the people or from the authorities, but especially the former. Thus sustenance is attitudinal. Maintenance, on the other hand, deals with the physical. These twin problems arise especially when sponsors, either national governments or donors, withdraw after the completion of a project. There are two solutions: to have the beneficiaries have a concrete stake in the project; and to involve local government at every stage and clearly define what its role will be after completion of the project.

Another major problem of rural development is the application and relevance of research. The SADCC region provides an example that one could easily extend to all the other regions of the continent. In this region, FAO studies reveal that there is a substantial amount of research output awaiting dissemination and application in the field. For instance, many technological solutions devised 10, 20, and even 30 years ago are still not widely applied. One important example is the creation of substitutes for bread ingredients. Research has shown that maize, rice, cassava, and soybean flour could be good substitutes for wheat flour in bread; the technology has been tested, but no application has followed. This leads to the question of relevance. In research of this type, the surprising thing is that local grains, such as millet and guinea corn, and tubers, which are the basis of food self-sufficiency, are not given adequate attention. Only recently has research on tubers been more than minimal.

The problem of irrelevance comes from the approach of researchers themselves. Farmers are a very large reservoir of knowledge, but they are usually ignored or even scorned. In the SADCC region research revealed that farmers developed input packages far more productive than those provided by the research stations. In Sudan, a plant called *cassia obtusifolia* has many important uses to the local people. It grows wild, even in areas affected by soil erosion and desertification, and supplies nutrients also obtained from meat and fish (Arthur). Its stems are used for building huts; its seeds cure jaundice; and tea from it provides a remedy for headaches and stomachaches; and during famine, people have survived on this plant. Yet Mr. Arthur found that little, if any, research has been done on it. There is a fount of knowledge ready to be tapped if only the researchers would stop ignoring the experience of the local people.

Another major problem of rural development is the very meager budget allocation or contribution made to the rural sector. The World Food Program is of the view that pledges made about increasing budgetary allocation to agriculture are just rhetoric. In the light of this statement, an FAO study on public expenditure on agriculture in African countries will be examined, first at the general level and then, drawing examples from a few countries, at the specific level. The FAO undertook a study of budgeted (planned) expenditure on agriculture in 57 LDCs, some in Africa, over the period 1978–82. The study found that the 57 countries allocated $125 billion dollars to agriculture in their public sector budgets. In 1978 constant dollars, the expenditure averaged only $20 billion per annum.

The details for Africa are as follows: Public expenditure as a percentage of GDP was 3.2 percent as compared with the average for the 57 countries, which was 3.0 percent. Ten out of 21 countries budgeted less than 10 percent of their agricultural GDP in 1978–82 for public expenditure on agriculture, and, for the countries for which data was available, only Benin, the Gambia, Kenya, and Somalia had a figure of more than 5 percent of GDP. In per capita terms, Egypt and Sudan budgeted only $7 and $10 respectively over the 1978–82 period. When it comes to the question of expenditure in real terms, the situation is gloomy. Eleven out of 21 countries had negative real annual growth rates for planned agricultural expenditure for 1978–82. The study reveals that African countries have been having the greatest difficulty in maintaining expenditure growth rates in both current and real terms: 12 of 19 countries had declining rates in real capital expenditure on agriculture, and 5 had declines in current terms. Seven of 9 LDCs in Africa had negative real growth rates for capital expenditure, but Gambia, Guinea, and Lesotho had annual growth rates of expenditure greater than 18 percent. On the other hand, Gabon was 1 of 14 countries in Africa that allocated less than 5 percent of its total public expenditure to agriculture. This again, as in the case of Congo and Nigeria, is not surprising, for Gabon is an oil economy importing around 80 percent of its food requirements. However, on the whole, the study revealed that the LDCs spent far less per capita than developed nations on agriculture.

At the specific or country level, I present data from nine countries. In Southern Africa, data for Botswana show that it allocates 90 percent of its budget to rural development programs, while subsidy to its arable land development program ranges from 30 to 80 percent. If these figures are correct, Botswana tops all African countries in its allocation of resources to the rural sector. Malawi, in the same region, allocates a hefty 40 percent of its annual budget to agriculture. Perhaps this explains why it is self-sufficient in food and is one of the three African countries, including Kenya and Zimbabwe, that are exporters of food. Kenya also allocates a substantial amount of its budget to agriculture. In the case of Zimbabwe, this phenomenon is explained by the presence of successful European farmers.

In Central Africa, Congo usually allocates 6 percent of its annual budget to the rural sector, and the government contribution to the rural development fund is 60 percent. In Zaire, budgetary allocation to agriculture and rural development was 2.5 percent in 1975, 8.7 percent in 1977, but down to 3.8 percent in 1981.

Five countries from West Africa are used here as examples. In 1984, out of the countries' total national budgets, Cape Verde allocated 25 percent of its budget to rural development; Senegal allocated 21 percent to the rural sector and contributed 20 percent to the rural fund; and Sierra Leone allocated 7.3 percent in 1975 and 8.2 percent in 1979–80 to agriculture and rural development. Burkina Faso usually budgeted 6 percent for the rural sector and contributed 10 percent to its rural fund; Togo allocated 42 percent to agriculture and 50 percent to the rural sector fund. This ranks Togo among the few African nations that allocate a very large proportion of their budget to agriculture.

The preceding figures for budgetary allocations to agriculture and rural development deserve some comment. First, the allocations are very meager relative to the importance of the rural sector, which forms the bedrock of all African economies. Second, most of the figures given by governments are those of budgeted (planned) expenditures, not actual expenditures. And given the formidable problems of implementing development programs in Africa, it is highly unlikely that they attain a 50 percent implementation level; where such an impressive level is reached, a closer examination will usually reveal that it is in terms of financial expenditure rather than physical attainment. Third, care should be taken in interpreting percentages because sometimes such an approach conceals low absolute figures. Sometimes this is true of increases: much depends on the base used.

Fourth, and most important, the proportion of budgetary allocations absorbed by administration should be noted. A particularly interesting example is Mali. The rural sector provides an estimated 70 percent of government's ordinary revenue. But on the negative side a hefty 90 percent of the national budget (98 percent in 1982) goes to maintain the civil service. Meantime, the proportion of government spending devoted to the rural sector never reached the 10 percent mark: it was a meager 2 percent in 1974 and 6.8 percent in 1976. It was the same story in Burkina Faso until recently. The civil service used to allocate to itself 65 percent of the budget while representing only 0.035 percent of the population. Both Mali and Burkina Faso are classic cases of exploitation. The rural sector is producing only to subsidize the civil service. This trend explains the size of the civil service in many countries. With respect to rural development there are two further examples: in Nigeria, until recently, the administrative cadre represented 40 percent of the total work force engaged in the rural development program; in Zaire the figure was as high as 90 percent.

The next important, though neglected, problem of rural development is losses arising from post-harvest handling of produce. Two examples from the SADCC region and Kenya have already been mentioned in chapter 3. An additional instance is Nigeria, where food losses from storage problems amount to 3 million tons annually. The neglect of this vital aspect of agriculture and rural development arises from a combination of complacency and folly. A small expenditure would help many African nations do away with food aid and food imports and thus perhaps even save billions of dollars in foreign exchange.

The major problems of rural development have been discussed in detail. But is there nothing but problems? Are there no instances of success? There are successes, at least in production. At the general level, in my view, any country that is self-sufficient in food is a success. At the specific level of achievement, three countries, namely Mali, Malawi, and Zambia, have succeeded in raising agricultural production at least in certain crops. In Mali there is a project, Mali-Sud, started in 1976 and financed by the International Development Association (IDA). As a result, cotton production went up 40 percent; farmers' revenue rose 30 percent in real terms, and output of cereals, especially maize, increased substantially. In Malawi, under the rural water supply schemes, 4,160 village taps were installed and by 1983 were serving 640,000 people. The villagers themselves installed 300 kilometers of pipes. The secret of success of this project was the involvement of the local people—chiefs, party leaders, and parliamentarians.

Zambia provides a more detailed example. In the first place, structural reforms raised crop output by 9 percent in 1984 and 1985. In the second place, detailed data are provided by Zambia's three integrated rural development projects, based in the northwestern, eastern, and northern provinces, which supplied packages of seed and fertilizers to farmers for cash and credit. An interesting aspect of the projects is that tractors were deliberately excluded and only hoes and ox plows were used. Yet the increases in ouput were tremendous. In the northwestern province, between 1979 and 1981, a time span of three years or less, output rose as follows: marketed maize, 180 percent; rice, 100 percent; sunflower, 60 percent; peanuts, 50 percent; and beans, 10 percent. In the eastern province the ouput of hybrid maize rose 60 percent in project areas compared with non-project areas. In the northern province yields of maize per hectare were 6.95 and 22.18 in 1974 and 1980-81 respectively.

These examples of a positive trend in production are signs of optimism for rural development. And the most noteworthy is Zambia's northwestern province's integrated rural development project, where only hoes and ox plows have been responsible for leaps in output. This means that modernized appropriate technology could bring about profound changes in production levels and thus in the lives of the rural populace. These examples demonstrate that what is required is political will and resources, but such resources must be deployed in a concentrated manner if positive results are to be achieved.

Lastly, the end of development is people. All efforts and resources are deployed for their welfare. Anyone who lives in an urban area knows the needs of urban dwellers, but with respect to rural dwellers, it is a different matter. But policymakers impose their notion of needs on the rural populace. They think they know without learning from the rural people. This is a mistake. To show this, two examples are presented here. In Malawi a survey revealed the rural felt needs such as health services, produce markets, primary schools, community halls, and water, the most needed are health services, water, and education. On the other hand, in Tanzania the situation is different. Rural needs are perceived in terms of incentive goods. A survey revealed that farmers preferred the following goods (in descending order): clothes, sugar, soap, cooking oil, kerosene, salt, matches, hoes, bicycles, and cement. And the most desired when income doubled were clothes, sugar, and soap (*Daily News*, June 17, 1986). The contrast in terms of rural needs between the two countries is sharp. In Malawi the needs emphasize social and infrastructural services; in Tanzania the emphasis is on consumer goods. The conclusion, presumably, then is that in Malawi consumer goods are available and accessible to the rural populace, but infrastructure is in short supply. In Tanzania it is the reverse. (I know the Tanzanian situation directly.) In its development strategy, Tanzania concentrated on the provision of health services, water, and education to rural dwellers, and consumer goods were very scarce until the second half of 1985.

The purpose of the two examples of rural felt needs is to underline the importance of at least conducting a survey of rural needs before designing rural development programs and projects.

6 *The Aid Trap*

The international community is watching and it will not make any significant move to assist us unless we effect the changes needed in production and mentality.

Ide Oumarou

Africa has chosen rural development as an alternative development strategy. This strategy has as its basis the principle of self-reliance. Yet Africa is the highest recipient of aid of all the developing continents in the world. The question then arises: How can one reconcile the principle of self-reliance with aid, for aid implies dependence and dependence negates self-reliance? This contradiction, in turn, raises further questions: Does aid help development? Or is aid good at a certain level and bad beyond it? Some argue that in fact aid is enervating.

Perhaps the best way to answer these questions is to measure the impact of aid, but probably few institutions engaged in development aid try to do so. The reasons may be many, but one may be outstanding: the difficulty of separating the impact of aid from the impact of development activities undertaken by the recipient with its own resources. Development effort entails an infinite number of activities and a flow of large quantities of resources. These activities are intertwined and form a complex web of relationships, hence the difficulty of isolating the impact of a set of activities, not to mention a single one. Yet at least a crude measure is possible. But such an exercise needs a clear baseline: there should be a measure of the situation that existed before the aid. Then, from the period of the aid, its contribution could be measured periodically. This would again require the difficult exercise of isolating, at least conceptually, the activities of aid from those of the recipient, for the two are carried out simultaneously.

The measurement of the impact of aid will entail the measurement of several, if not many variables. The most obvious are economic and welfare variables, at least as a start. Measures would have to be constructed of how much aid has contributed to economic variables such as the growth rate of the economy, to the GDP, to agricultural and industrial productivity, and to the advance in technology, just to mention a few. On the side of welfare, the measurement would concern itself with factors such as health conditions, life expectancy, infant and child mortality, water supply, sanitation, and other items of social infrastructure. But this is just one aspect of measuring the impact of aid; there is another very important one, self-reliance. Aid is presumably given to help the recipient to attain self-reliance at some time in the future. Therefore, the question then arises: In spite of aid's impressive contribution to economic growth and welfare conditions, has it reduced the recipient's dependence on the donor? In other words, has aid promoted self-reliance? It is when the answers to these questions are positive that one can say aid has been useful; otherwise it would play a negative role in the recipient's struggle for self-reliance.

I have dwelt on the question of measuring the impact of aid because of its importance in connection with the principle of self-reliance, which Africa has accepted as the foundation of its development strategy. Therefore it is very important for Africa to know whether aid promotes or negates the struggle for self-reliance. In addition, the debate as to the usefulness of aid is currently raging in the donor countries and multilateral institutions. Aid institutions, whether national or multinational, have taken the position that aid is serving a useful purpose, and a few of them have started collecting statistics to demonstrate the validity of their position. On the other side of the argument are some citizens of the donor countries who maintain that aid has not been of use at all. In this debate the academicians occupy the middle ground. As of now, no one can tell who will win, but what is certain is that there are signs of aid fatigue, a phenomenon that will be discussed in detail below. Meantime, Africa should study the trend very carefully and prepare itself for the worst eventuality in terms of aid flows. Africa relishes aid, but the prevailing mood and trend show that it should not be surprised when the flow declines drastically. The complete drying up of aid is ruled out because those who give it have their own ends, which are served by aid. And unless aid ceases completely to serve a useful purpose for them, which is unlikely, it will continue to flow. Nonetheless, when there is heavy dependence on aid, even a marginal cut in it will entail some painful readjustment in the recipient country.

With this background I will discuss three aspects of aid, namely reasons for giving it, its forms and flows to Africa, and aid fatigue and the aid trap.

REASONS FOR GIVING AID

Aid and loans perform similar, if not the same, functions. Loans are given to create or provide markets for goods and services. They are also given to stimulate new markets and orient national economies toward free enterprise. Aid does the same. The main difference is that a loan carries interest and aid does not. But even in this respect, there are institutions that call their loans aid. This is presumably because the loans are so soft that they are like aid.

Another difference between aid and loans is that the former has a stronger element of technical assistance, in two forms. In one the donor provides personnel directly to implement and run a project for some time before the local people take over the management responsibility. In the other, the donor trains manpower in various fields for the recipient. But even in loan agreements both elements exist, though in less obvious forms. For instance, a loan may be contracted to implement a project with the aim of promoting or orienting the economy toward private enterprise. In such an arrangement, again two things happen. In the first place, the lender's personnel participate in managing the enterprise, usually at the top. In fact, in extreme cases, the whole management of the enterprise is contracted and a management fee paid—an effective form of leakage of resources, including profits and debt service. In the second place, and less important, private enterprises usually arrange for the training of some middle- and lower-level personnel in the parent company. This does not usually involve a substantial number of people.

In addition, one must return to the matter of interest. Interest promotes dependence: the burden of debt eliminates any room for maneuver. Aid does not have such a constraint on the recipient because it is given of the volition of the donor. Thus the only way the recipient could mortgage its freedom is by relying too heavily on the aid, but the recipient has the freedom to minimize this reliance and thus protect its freedom.

I also implied the other difference between aid and a loan when I pointed out that a loan entails leakages of resources from the recipient country in the form of profits, debt service, and remittances of the personnel working in the recipient nation. This does not take into account sharp practices in imports, exports, and pricing. In imports and exports, overinvoicing accounts for huge leakages of foreign exchange and other resources of the recipient country. Similarly, the technique of pricing is used by multinational giants to transfer resources from one country to another. These corporations have many branches all over the world, and each trades among its branches, transferring raw materials and finished products among them. It is while arranging such trades that they fix prices that give them the greatest profit. Inputs are bought cheaply in one country and shipped to another country that levies no tax on them; manufactures are produced in that country and sold expensively to branches of the same multinational in other countries, perhaps including the one from which the inputs originated. It is an intricate game, and it is only the international finance and trading "wizards" who are conversant with such tricks. They have to be because they live cheaply only on such tricks. No wonder they guard such secrets. Not only are the tricks illegal but with knowledge about the tricks a swarm of competitors would threaten their livelihood.

It may be tempting to conclude that aid should surely be preferred to loans because it does not entail such leakages. The reasons for such a conclusion would be that profits, debt servicing, overinvoicing, management contracts, and other sharp practices are not involved in aid. It is true that many practices associated with private enterprise are not found in aid programs. But aid has its own type of leakages. In this regard, the first thing to remember is that aid is tied and therefore there is some ulterior motive attached to it. This phenomenon is discussed below as a caveat to the conclusion that aid is completely innocent. There is no completely innocent aid; all aid has some sort of strings. These may be purely or partly economic, such as the promotion or creation of markets. They may be military, in which case military bases, support, or intervention could be sought against a third country of different ideological or economic orientation. The strings may also be political; for example, the donor country might seek to influence the voting behavior of the recipient country in the UN and its agencies. Therefore the possibility of innocent aid is ruled out. What differs here is the relative strength of the string. Some nations may make the string very strong, to the point of blackmail, and thus effectively curtail the sovereignty of the recipient. Other countries make the strings weak. In this category are the Nordic countries and, to some extent, the socialist countries. But what these countries are doing is playing the game of foresight: they cultivate friendship now for a reward in the future, as far into the future as a quarter of a century, or even beyond. This makes eminent good sense because all industrialized countries have more or less completely exhausted their natural resources. Some, like Japan, from the beginning did not have the natural resource base to support the huge industrial structure of the twentieth century. Meantime, there are parts of the world where natural resources have hardly been exploited. Countries in these parts of the world have been feeding the global industrial machinery with resources for centuries, and they are still doing so. Competition for resources among the industrial nations is getting fiercer every day, and this is already threatening a nuclear holocaust. If the global community succeeds in averting nuclear disaster and resources are to be exploited peacefully, then friendship between countries that have natural resources and those that do not will become crucial for access to these resources. This is the friendship that some wiser countries are cultivating now so as to ensure the flow of resources to their industries. Of course, one should not underrate the role of science and technology in providing solutions to the rapid depletion or even exhaustion of resources. That is why scientists are aiming for the moon and other planets with the hope of discovering resources. But this is a long-term and very costly solution pursued at the expense of hungry, diseased, and dying millions on this small globe. Moreover, the rapidity with which resources are being depleted will, if not checked, bring about catastrophe long before scientific and technological solutions become available to avert it.

Some argue that there is no altruism in aid. This is not an empty argument, and in support of it I offer three examples: (1) the type of project many donors are interested in; (2) the amount of benefit derived from aid by donors, with the particular example of the United States; and (3) the growing militarization of aid, again with the example of the United States.

Aid takes many forms, but whatever the form, it entails the formulation and implementation of projects. The question then is: What size of project? Are they a few big projects that benefit both the donor and the urban power elite, or are they a large number of small projects that are designed to benefit the rural poor? In most cases, at least perhaps until recently, projects have been of the big, elitist, urban-biased type. The reasons for choosing such projects are many, but three are immediately obvious: the type of beneficiaries, the political impact on the people, and the size of resource leakage.

The power elite makes the policy decision about projects, and therefore the chances are high that it will choose those that benefit it most. It derives two immediate benefits. First, such projects are designed to produce luxury consumption goods to which only the elite have access. The second benefit is associated with corruption in the form of kickbacks. Admittedly, this happens more in the case of private enterprise than in the case of aid projects, but one cannot rule out the possibility of corruption on the part of those who have won the contract to execute the project. This happens at both the bidding and implementation stages. In implementation it happens when deliberate bureaucratic obstacles are put in the way of the contractors. In this game, the local bourgeois compradors are not left out: they derive benefit from the crumb, which come to them by way of subcontracting. They are given contracts to supply a particular material; if it is available locally, the local comprador gains from supplying it.

On the clamor for big projects, Michael Tanzer has made some penetrating observations. On the pressure to invest he observed that members of the ruling elite in oil- and mineral-exporting countries have a relatively short time horizon because they do not expect to stay in power for long (*Monthly Review*, April 1984). This is true, but I would say the attitude is not confined to those countries; it applies to most Third World countries, especially the most unstable ones or those where political changes are rapid. The ruling elite tries to make as much as possible before being replaced by another ruling elite. The more rapid the investment and the larger the projects, the greater the benefits derived by the ruling elite and the local bourgeois comprador.

Tanzer also commented on the bureaucracy's preference for large-scale projects, noting that large projects harmonize with the tendency of the bureaucracies to build bigger empires (*Monthly Review*, April 1984). This enables them to obtain a bigger share, in the form of higher salaries, perquisites, power, and prestige, of the surplus accumulated by the state.

A second major benefit derived from large-scale projects is what I call the political benefit, which derives from the visibility of the project. In Third World countries, especially in Africa, development is synonymous with structures even if they are white elephants. The politicians are able to show them to the people as a concrete sign of progress and development. This provides the politicians with a campaign tool to win the next election and return to power.

So far, only the side of the recipient has been considered as far as large-scale projects are concerned. But how does the donor view them? The donor nation or institution views the projects from two perspectives, their visibility and the opportunities they offer for leakage. This illusion is shared with the ruling elite. The donor can cite the projects as a reflection of that country's contribution to development. Leakage from large-scale projects comes about through the involvement of contractors from the donor country, and large-scale projects provide lucrative work. Contractors earn profits; they also remit home the salaries and wages of their workers. Meantime, after completion of a large-scale project, the benefit to the recipient becomes questionable. A good example, but only one of many scattered all over the globe, is a dam project in Sri Lanka. The four-hundred-foot-high Victoria Dam was built with British government aid of £100 million, one of the largest grants ever made. It was stipulated that the dam be built by British firms. It was expected to cost £136 million, but its final cost was £250 million (*Appropriate Technology*, Vol. 13 No. 1 June, 1986). The Sri Lankans ended up paying one and one-half times the aid to get the dam completed. Yet the story does not end here. The dam displaced 45,000 people when 6 towns and 123 villages were submerged. It also cost several schools, a prison, 14 Buddhist temples, and, most serious, 1,000 acres of Sri Lanka's most fertile rice-growing land.

I have discussed the type of projects donors are interested in along with reasons for their interest. I have shown that the reasons are mainly pecuniary, but there is also, to a lesser extent, pride in contributing to the economic and social development of the recipient country. Now, by way of detail, I discuss a concrete example of the magnitude of benefits derived by the donor. As I mentioned, earlier, this example is the United States.

Before World War II the United States had great economic power. It was self-sufficient in virtually all resources and was advancing rapidly industrially and technologically. World War II did not affect the United States much, for it was not a theater of war. So, before the war ended the United States had the foresight to plan the control of the global economic system. This was discussed in detail in chapter 3. However, one thing that was not in doubt was the hegemony that the United States had over the global system before it was challenged by the Soviet Union, West Germany, Japan, and now Europe as a unit. While this challenge was growing, the United States was becoming more and more dependent on world trade. Resources were shrinking and competition was sharpening; autarchy was no longer possible. The magnitude of the growing United States dependence on or immersion in the world trading system is underscored by the following statistics: By the early 1970s one out of every seven people employed in the United States was employed as a result of trading with the LDCs, and about 35 percent of U.S. exports went to the LDCs. These are large figures even by U.S. standards, not to mention the LDCs. In addition to the huge trading flows, one-third of the profits of U.S. firms was earned in the LDCs—again, by all standards, a huge figure. In absolute terms, it would run into billions of dollars. There is also ground for supposing that this figure has since risen sharply for various reasons, the most obvious of which are the rising costs of manufactures and the placing of a burden of debt on the developing countries. The latter alone generates billions of dollars in debt service for the United States.

It should be remembered that both debt and aid have the function of stimulating and creating markets for goods and services. And here is a situation where the United States is becoming more and more dependent on global trade, reaping greater benefits from it, perhaps, than any other country. This shows that it is in the interest of the United States to give aid even for economic or commercial reasons alone. Yet in recent years the United States has been cutting its aid. In 1982 an American economist became curious about this development; he could not understand why the United States should cut back aid when it, rather than the recipients, is the actual beneficiary from aid giving. He made some calculations and arrived at the conclusion that for every dollar the United States gave in aid, it received back two dollars and fifty-four cents. The difference is a hefty one and a half dollars. It is indeed difficult to explain this contradiction. How could a country that gains from aid spearhead the campaign to cut back on it? In economic parlance, such behavior is irrational. But there must be convincing reasons for it. What are they? At best, one could only speculate.

It is significant that there is no evidence of pressure or complaints against aid by the people of the United States. The negative attitude is on the part of the government, probably for two reasons, the arms build-up and blackmail. The government of the United States either has convinced itself that it is genuinely at a disadvantage in the arms race with the Soviet Union; or is using this alleged disadvantage as an excuse to gain superiority in the arms race or to stimulate a slumping economy. Or it may be doing both of these. However, there is no doubt that the United States has been losing its dominance over the world in the last few decades. Therefore it feels, erroneously, that only a show of force can restore its hegemonic position. Hence the tremendous arms build-up currently going on in the United States. What has this got to do with aid? Perhaps the aid cutback will save some dollars for the arms build-up.

A second possible reason for cutting aid is blackmail. Aid, especially where it is substantial, encourages dependence. The recipient's freedom is effectively curtailed, and it must execute the will of the aid giver or else the aid is cut in order to make the recipient behave. And in recent years, the United States has been facing challenges not only from Europe and Japan but also from the developing countries. The challenges from Europe and Japan are economic, and those from the LDCs are political and are usually expressed at the level of the UN and its agencies. There is no doubt that the former are more serious to the United States than the latter. But on the other hand, the significance of the political challenge is that it might swing the sympathy of other industrialized countries toward the Third World. The United States would do all in its power to prevent this, hence it twists arms by cutting back on aid.

To return to reasons for giving aid, a major one is military interests. As far back as the early 1970s, the United States had 1,400 foreign military bases in more than 31 countries; and it is far more likely for the number to have increased by now than to have decreased. The reasons for having military bases are well known, and military aid is a very important component of aid given by the United States and other countries having similar interests. In fact, though United States aid in general has in recent years decreased in absolute terms, the military component has simultaneously been increasing. For instance, in 1981, of the total U.S. aid budget of $9 billion, "security" aid, a euphemism for military aid, claimed 51 percent. In 1985 security aid absorbed 67 percent of the total aid budget of $14 billion. The trend is clear. With the arms control negotiations going on with the Soviet Union, the proportion of security aid is more likely than not to continue rising.

A further important aspect of aid that African countries, and indeed the developing world, should appreciate, is the relationship of aid to efforts to industrialize. What is the policy of aid donors toward industries? I do not have information as to their attitude toward giving direct aid to locally owned industrial enterprises. But toward public enterprises, the policy is clear: aid agencies have declined to finance them. Until recently, public institution building was an important aspect of aid because it was realized that lack of efficient public administration was one of the major obstacles to development. And in the 1970s and 1980s, aid was directed largely to intermediate credit institutions serving private enterprises. There are two questions to raise here. First, who owns the intermediate credit institutions? Second, who owns the private enterprises? Are both wholly locally owned or are they partnerships? The answer is that these institutions are highly unlikely to be owned by the local petty bourgeoisie. The reality usually is that some are partnerships, with the the local partner on the weaker side, and others are wholly foreign-owned. In both cases the channels of leakage are clear: the aid goes back to where it came from with great gains. Therefore, the use of this form of aid is highly questionable, except in the training of personnel of wholly locally owned credit institutions and enterprises.

The refusal to aid state industrial enterprises is understandable. I have mentioned several times that one of the fundamental reasons for giving aid is the stimulation of existing markets and the development of new ones whereby the donor will gain. Both the parent company and its branches in the recipient country will gain from the benefits offered by the recipient's market. But with public enterprises, there is no such gain. There are two reasons for this. First, public enterprises are owned by the government and, by implication, by the citizens of the country concerned. In these enterprises resources are generated and used in the country. In short, resources are recycled domestically and therefore retained in the country. Second, public enterprises, when well developed, will compete effectively with foreign enterprises operating either locally or abroad. This will generate competition for resources and markets. In both cases, public enterprises will be aided by their owner, the government, in capturing the market and having easy access to resources. In addition, domestic industrialization will cut the supply of raw materials to the industrialized countries. Hence the deliberate effort to delay the industrialization of the LDCs. Therefore, it is not surprising that donors refused to support the proposed global Fund for Industrialization.

In the end, says Joan Robinson, aid is merely an allocation of foreign exchange finance, but not stock of production capital. And, in fact, I have shown that even where stock of capital is allocated, insofar as it is associated with foreign contracting firms, it hardly makes any difference because of the huge leakages of resources.

THE TYPES AND FLOWS OF AID TO AFRICA

In the previous section the donors' reasons for giving aid were analyzed. In this section the side of the recipient is discussed in terms of both the types and the flows of aid. The general African situation, the statistics of the flow of aid, the types of aid, and examples from a few countries are examined, and I suggest which is the best type of aid.

There are many types of aid, but at a very general level, it may be categorized into "technical" and "other." Within the two broad categories there is a large number of subcategories. Those within the technical assistance category would seem to be fewer and hence easier to handle. In the "other" category there are many subdivisions. However, my main concern here does not warrant a detailed categorization of aid. A few examples of subcategories will be sufficient.

Technical assistance has mainly to do with personnel and is of two types. In one, the donor supplies personnel or experts to an institution or a project while it is being executed. They are expected to give on-the-job training to citizens of the recipient nation within a usually specified period of time with a view to handing management over to the recipient. In the other type of technical assistance, the donor trains manpower in some areas of need for the recipient country. How, when, and where the training is to be done are usually matters agreed upon by the parties concerned.

Technical assistance may include institution building, the rationale being that it concerns personnel. Institution building has two main elements, the design of the structure of the institution and the provision of the personnel. This latter aspect entails a training program which is usually the main concern of technical assistance.

Consultancy is another form of technical assistance. Over the last two decades, consultancy as a specialized activity has increased tremendously and it still maintains its popularity with all types of institutions, both public and private. Hence it is an important form of technical assistance.

These three examples of technical assistance may not exhaust the types. For example, assistance to credit institutions may fall within this category. Nonetheless, the three types that I have mentioned cover almost all that is expected of technical assistance.

The second broad category of aid, which I have named "other," has many subcategories, and therefore I will give only a few examples and identify them by the type of aid. In doing so, I use the sectors of the economy as a means of classification, just as development plans usually do.

But as a preliminary, let me point out that various countries have different sectoral divisions of their economy. For example, for purposes of planning, Nigeria divides its economy into four broad sectors: economic, social, general administration, and regional development. Some nations may have a greater number of divisions, for instance, dividing the social sector into social services and infrastructural services to form two sectors. Others may add sectors such as energy, technology, and so on. The division of the economy into sectors depends, among many other things, on priorities and the availability of reliable statistical data, which facilitates detailed planning.

Aid may be given to any sector of the economy. In the economic sector, which is usually considered to be the directly productive one, aid might be channeled to agriculture or industry, or both; in the social sector it could be channeled to the subsectors of health, education, roads, water, and so on. Other sectors may be subdivided in a similar way.

Africa has received aid in a variety of subsectors. However, the most important thing is not which sector received what but the magnitude of the aid itself and its implications for Africa's freedom. It has already been argued that aid is enervating and promotes subservience. Yet Africa is the greatest receiver of aid in the world—to the tune of $20 per head as compared with all other LDCs, which receive $12 per head. The situation is more alarming when it is noted that Africa depends on aid for more than 50 percent of its gross domestic investment and 40 percent of its total imports. It is worthwhile at this stage to take a critical look of this alarming level of dependency.

Investment is the root of growth. Savings provide the surplus needed for investment, which, in turn, by promoting growth, is the basis for generating future surplus. When Africa depends on aid for 50 percent of its gross domestic investment, it simply means mortgaging its growth machine to some other country or a foreign institution, which then has the power to control and orient the growth machine as it wishes. It should be clear that the donor will orient investment toward its own interests, not those of the recipient. It is usually in the donor's interests that Africa does not industrialize, at least not rapidly, for if that were to happen, the donor country or institution would lose markets and raw materials. Hence Africa must remain a market and a source of raw materials.

Fifty percent of gross domestic investment consists of two parts, the one owned by local citizens and the government, the other owned by foreign interests. Even the locally owned part is forced to depend on the foreign-owned enterprises. This dependence takes several forms, for instance, supplies of critical inputs and subcontracting where the local enterprises are strong enough. Where they are not strong, even subcontracts go to foreign firms. Therefore, usually, the part owned by foreign interests is the stronger and more powerful because it has greater resources and has succeeded in creating an island of efficiency. This means that it controls the engine of growth and thus the whole economy.

Dependence on aid for 40 percent of total imports is an obvious danger. Africa depends almost wholly on imports for its development programs and even its consumer goods. Anything, from critical industrial inputs, machinery, and spare parts to a needle, is imported. And Africa could finance only 60 percent of such imports from its internally generated resources. In addition, the bulk of the imported industrial inputs, machinery and spare parts, is claimed by the foreign enterprises located in the country. This is another side of dependency.

A combination of a high level of dependence on external resources for gross domestic investment and imports makes meaningful planning impossible for two main reasons. The first is that the flow of aid is highly uncertain and hence erratic; the second is that, even if the aid flows in steadily, the powerful foreign interests in the economy can subtly subvert any planning strategies that are not in their favor. To do this, they can even resort to blackmail, at the risk of expulsion, knowing that they are too vital to the economy to be expelled. These factors, in addition to the volatile global environment, make planning impossible. The stable environment that is a prerequisite for planning does not exist. Given the high dependence on foreign resources for investments and imports, it is no wonder that Africa has found itself in greater dependency than any region in the world.

The relationship between planning and aid reminds one of the experience of two countries that relied heavily on aid when they formulated their initial development plans. These countries are Nigeria and Tanzania. Nigeria, in its 1962–68 development plan, planned for almost 50 percent of the resources to come from external sources, namely aid. That was a very unrealistic calculation, and therefore, it is not surprising that the dream was never realized. The result was that it led to a low level of plan implementation. In the next plan, Nigeria seemed to have learned its lesson, but one cannot be sure whether it was for this reason or something else. The reason for scepticism is that, by the time Nigeria formulated its second development plan, the oil money was flowing, and hence the need for aid was eliminated. On the other hand, it might have been that even without oil money, Nigeria would have been at least a bit more careful concerning aid in formulating its second development plan.

Tanzania has made the same mistake as Nigeria. In planning its development expenditure, it has relied heavily on foreign aid, to the extent that at one time it became the highest recipient of aid per capita in Africa and, by extension, the world. Foreign aid has always accounted for over 50 percent of Tanzania's development expenditure. The problem of such heavy reliance is the contradiction between such dependence and self-reliance: Tanzania is the greatest proponent of the principle of self-reliance, and yet it is the greatest recipient of aid per capita. Perhaps the argument for heavy reliance on aid is that aid would give a push to development and thus help in promoting self-reliance. But observation does not show that things have worked this way. In fact, there seem to be some signs that aid has worked in the opposite way in Tanzania; it has enervated the country in its development efforts. The country is very rich in resources, but it is almost wholly unexploited. This then raises the question: Where has the aid gone? The answer belongs to another aspect of aid, namely its utilization. Unfortunately, it is a question with which I am not conerned here. But it is an interesting question that needs to be studied. It is to be hoped that scholars will take it up. Whatever the case, donors in Tanzania are beginning to ask, "Where has the aid gone?" This could as well be asked of all those nations receiving aid, especially those that rely heavily on it and have been receiving it for a long time.

There are four other African countries that depend heavily on aid: Lesotho, Kenya, the Ivory Coast, and Cameroon. Of these, Lesotho has one of the highest flows of aid in the world on a per capita basis. The intention behind making Cameroon a heavy aid recipient is not clear to me. But as to Kenya and the Ivory Coast, it does seem that the intention is to make them capitalist showcases, that is, islands of capitalist success and hence superiority. There are two fundamental reasons for donors to adopt this strategy. One, mentioned earlier, is to orient economies toward the capitalist system. In this respect, the two countries may have been chosen to serve as models of the success of the capitalist system. They are then expected to be examples to other nations. Thus the two would serve as effective propaganda instruments for spreading the capitalist system in Africa. Whether this strategy has succeeded or not, or whether there are chances of success in the future, is something else with which I am not concerned here. But one thing to remember is this: *Newsweek* magazine had a feature article on the Ivorian economy. It analyzed in detail the various sectors of the economy, especially the economic sector. But even here it focused mainly on growth to show how impressively the economy had performed over the years. Nothing was mentioned about the distribution of wealth and income, not even the distribution of enterprises between the local comprador bourgeoisie and foreign interests. But it is commonly known that the Ivorian economy is controlled by the French. Even stores are owned by foreigners. This aspect of the Ivorian economy will be discussed presently. For the moment, suffice it to say that the *Newsweek* article was designed as a propaganda piece to portray the Ivorian capitalist model as a successful one worth emulating by all countries.

The other reason for making the Ivory Coast and Kenya capitalist showcases is the structure of the ownership of wealth. This is a fundamental and interesting question. Both countries have a colonial heritage: the Ivory

Coast was and is still French, and Kenya was and is still, to a considerable extent, British. In the Ivory Coast, if the French own even the stores, then it follows that they have a firm grip on the productive sector of the economy, namely agriculture and industry. In agriculture they could easily own plantations that provide the industrial raw materials; in industry they own the factories. But in the ownership of stores the French are not alone; they are joined by the Lebanese and/or Syrians. Therefore, perhaps except for the subsistence agricultural sector, the Ivorian economy is wholly foreign-owned and controlled. It is also clear that the stakes for the French are high. Therefore, the major reason for the desire to project the Ivory Coast as a successful capitalist model is pecuniary interests.

There is a striking similarity between Kenya and the Ivory Coast as far as the ownership and control of the economy is concerned. Kenya was a British colony, and therefore, it is reasonable to expect the British to retain interests there. But there is an additional element to the Kenya situation—the presence of Asians. This presence has a historical explanation: A long time ago during the slave trade, first Arabs and then Asians established themselves along the eastern and southern coasts of Africa. These are, in the main, citizens of the countries where they settled. This is the main difference between the Ivory Coast and Kenya. In the Ivory Coast the presence of Lebanese or Syrian Arabs is a relatively recent phenomenon, and it is unlikely that they have acquired citizenship. On the other hand, many of the French are citizens of the Ivory Coast. Whatever the differences between the two, in Kenya as in the Ivory Coast the economy is owned and controlled by foreigners. The major foreign interests in Kenya are the British and the Americans, who have even established a military presence there. The citizens of those two nations own the major industries and perhaps even some of the medium-scale ones, including no doubt the major financial institutions such as banks and insurance companies. Arabs and Asians also have some interests in the financial system, but their presence is not as strong as that of the British and the Americans. Nonetheless, again in this respect, the stakes for the British and the Americans are high.

The case of the Asians in Kenya is different but presents the same problem of distribution of wealth. At least most, if not all, of them are citizens. They own almost all, if not all, the stores; a few of them probably own some medium-scale industries; but surely almost all the small industries are Asian-owned. So, what of the black Kenyans? They are subsistence farmers, workers in the public services and private enterprises, and employees in the stores owned by Asians. This pattern of income and wealth distribution presents for Kenya a special problem, which it shares with Uganda and Tanzania. In Uganda, when Idi Amin was in power, he took drastic and perhaps unwise action in expelling the Asians in 1972. On the other hand, Tanzania appears to have successfully contained the problem. There is a need to learn from the Tanzanian approach because the problem has a racial undertone and it could be explosive if not handled with care.

Having discussed at length the magnitude of flows of aid to Africa and their implications, one must look briefly at another aspect of aid, the statistics. Of course, it is understood that Africa has been receiving aid for many years; however, the statistics in my example are for 1984 only. In addition, they are only from donor agencies. Aid channeled through UN agencies, though perhaps greater, has not been included because it has less direct and adverse implications for control and dependency. This is not to deny that such control, and even blackmail, exists in the multinational agencies; it is not perpetrated by the agencies themselves but by contributors. Good examples are the United States and the United Kingdom, which withdrew from UNESCO and thus occasioned a drastic cut in its budget. Also, when the United States threatened to withhold all or much of its contribution to the UN, the institution was threatened with the prospect of being unable to pay the salaries of its staff. This is a clear example of arm-twisting.

There is a very large number of countries and donor agencies that provide aid to Africa and Third World nations elsewhere. Examples are the Overseas Development Association (ODA); the Commonwealth Development Corporation (CDC); the OPEC Fund for International Development; and the Soviet Union.

In 1984 the ODA gave Africa south of the Sahara a total of $322 million, covering a variety of countries and projects. A few available details show that from the CDC, Kenya got $5.2 million and another $8.45 million for agricultural supplies; Sudan received $4.9 million for farming projects; Cameroon and Zimbabwe each received $2.6 million; and $1.3–$2 million was shared by Zambia, the Ivory Coast, Malawi, and Liberia. Other recipients of aid from the ODC were Lesotho, Botswana, Swaziland, Tanzania, Somalia, Mauritius, Seychelles, Ghana, and the Gambia. Much of the aid has been for agriculture and livestock projects.

Similarly, in 1984 the CDC disbursed $52 million to projects in Africa, and the OPEC fund directly provided soft loans and other forms of aid valued at $15.50 million. The fund, in addition to providing International Fund for Agricultural Development (IFAD) with the initial capital of $861.1 million, channeled to Africa through various UN agencies aid totaling $128.60 million. The fund is also granting £500,000 toward a £30 million African fertilizer development center to be established in Harare, Zimbabwe, over a five-year period.

On the other hand, Soviet aid seems to have been mainly in the form of training, which, if costed, will surely amount to a substantial figure. Available statistics for Soviet aid are for all developing countries, but one may assume that Africa has been receiving a substantial amount of it. In the LDCs the Soviet Union has established technical and vocational training schools and centers, some of them at the university level. Over the years the Soviet Union has trained 590,000 people in Africa, Asia, and Latin America. Meanwhile, it has in the pipeline a project involving 407 vocational training centers, 250 of which are already operational. It also established a very important institute, the Petroleum Training Institute in Warri, Nigeria.

The Western industrialized countries have been providing aid in a large number of subsectors of the African economy, while the Soviet Union seems to have limited itself to the narrow aspect of training, except for a few large-scale projects involving dams and heavy industry.

There are two important observations about aid from the socialist bloc. Though the amount is small relative to what is offered by the West, it has the advantages of emphasizing training and being relatively free of blackmail and arm-twisting. A good example of magnanimity and tolerance was shown by the Soviet Union when its citizens were expelled from Egypt during the presidency of the late Anwar Sadat. They helped build the huge Aswan Dam and were at the time training and equipping the Egyptian army. It is highly unlikely that any Western country could have helped Egypt undertake such a huge and crucial project as the Aswan Dam. In Nigeria, the West refused to execute the country's largest and most important project, in iron and steel, though it would have made a huge profit from it. Western oil companies refused to pay royalties and governments refused to sell arms to the Nigerian military government during the Nigerian civil war. In the case of both the iron and steel project and the sales of arms, again it was the Soviet Union that came to the rescue of Nigeria.

But in comparison, it is important to recall the attitude of the French toward Guinea. When Guinea rejected membership in the French community in 1958, the French removed everything they thought was theirs from Guinea including, reportedly, school desks. It was so mean of a power such as France, but it was done. Compare this with Soviet equanimity when it was expelled from Egypt during the time of Sadat. The Soviets cannot of course remove a dam, but there were many other things they could have removed or done. These examples show that Africa should start to distinguish between aid givers by their attitude to Africa's progress. Those countries that are not prepared to undertake projects, even on a commercial basis, that are critical to Africa's development should be told to keep their aid.

AID FATIGUE AND THE AID TRAP

Aid has been a feature of global economic transactions probably for centuries. Recent trends in aid flows, whether bilaterally or through multinational agencies, tend to reveal a negative attitude toward aid. There are probably three fundamental reasons. The first is the global economic recession that has lasted for more than a decade and has adversely affected the performance of the economies of the donor nations. Consequently, the ability to give aid has declined, but, more important, the recession has reduced the welfare of the citizens of the industrialized countries. Thus opposition to aid is a foregone conclusion; it may be open or latent, but all the same, it exists. The second probable reason for the decline of aid is what may be called aid fatigue. Apart from the argument that aid helps governments to avoid making hard and unpleasant policies, questions are being asked as to what positive impact aid makes on the recipients. A report by the Organization for Economic Cooperation and Development (OECD) says that development aid has made a limited measurable contribution to the reduction of extreme poverty. But on the other hand, the report also claims that much has been achieved, with little assistance, in the areas of research, economic policy analysis, and training of key officials. However, as I indicated earlier, the problem of measuring the impact of aid is a real one, and until it is resolved, the citizens of donor countries will continue to ask the same question. They may or may not be aware that donor countries give aid for other reasons than helping the development of the recipients. Aid can be given purely for military and political reasons, and such objectives are attained when the recipient is made subservient. Hence the third probable reason for cutting aid, blackmail or arm-twisting. This is true especially of those countries that depend heavily on aid. A cutback occasions very painful adjustment, if indeed the will and means to adjust exist. Whatever the case, the painful process of adjustment might bring about social unrest or even political instability.

In recent years, aid fatigue has become a reality. The negative attitude to aid displayed in the UN agencies has been strongly influenced by the U.S. position, one intended to twist the arms of the LDCs for military and political reasons. Donors have reduced their contributions to many UN agencies, consequently compelling them to reduce their scale of operations. A few examples follow.

The negative attitude of the United States toward aid was expressed for the first time at the highest policymaking level at the Cancun summit meeting in 1981. The summit was called with a view to helping to solve North-South problems, but the spirit of the summit was killed by President Reagan, and to date nothing has been heard of the North-South dialogue expect on paper. And even on paper the enthusiasm for promoting understanding seems to have petered out because the industrialized countries would not hear of such a thing as a North-South dialogue. Perhaps the thinking is that a degree of arm-twisting will solve the problem, hence the prevailing negative attitude toward aid.

Aid targets agreed at the multinational level have never been met. It was agreed that the industrialized countries should contribute 0.7 percent of their GNP as their official development assistance to the LDCs. So far, only five countries have attained this target. For the rest, the average had been about 0.37 percent as recently as 1983, as compared with 0.51 percent in 1960 (Nyerere 1985). The declining trend is continuing, and this is evident in the contributions to the UN agencies.

Take, for example, the IDA, the soft loan arm of the World Bank. Sometime in 1985, IDA – 7 projected a level of contributions of $12 billion, but resistance from the United States brought down the amount to only $9 billion, a figure 25 percent and 40 percent lower in nominal and real terms respectively than IDA – 6 three years before. In another example the IBRD intended to raise over $2 billion for its Special Facility for Africa. It ended up with a meager $1.2 billion, again because of U.S. resistance to the plan. Efforts to rectify these setbacks continued: there were initiatives from the IMF and IDA – 8. The IMF revealed a new plan for a trust fund of 53 billion for "growth-oriented" LDCs at an interest rate of only 0.5 percent for the next three years. Meantime, IDA – 8 planned to raise contributions to $12 billion, the level intended for IDA – 7 (*African Business*, July 1986). Both the IMF and the IDA intentions are expected to meet resistance from the United States. In addition, it is also significant that the planned IMF trust fund, though very soft, is intended for growth-oriented LDCs, not for the poorest ones who need it most. The aim is clear: to promote market economies rather than to help the needy.

There is yet another example of the declining trend in aid, the United Nations Industrial Development Organization (UNIDO). This institution obtained a pledge of $50 million for its programs for 1985. But of this only $12.9 million, a meager 25.8 percent, was realized. To judge from developments in sister organizations, the trend in UNIDO is also likely to be downward.

The above analysis of trends in aid and the reasons for them reveals that there is more to the negative than the positive side of aid. The aims of donors are clear: to promote market economies and dependence so that LDCs will remain, at least for a long time, suppliers of raw materials and markets for manufactures of the industrial world; and through military and political aid to create dependence, with recipients of necessity becoming subservient.

Similarly, the intention of donors to keep recipients dependent for a long time is reflected in two examples given earlier, the refusal of donors to endorse the establishment of the world industrial fund; and the refusal of the Western industrialized countries to build Nigeria's iron and steel factory even on a commercial basis.

In addition to the above negative aspects, there have so far been no convincing measurements of the positive impact of aid on recipient economies, especially in the distribution of wealth and income and in raising the welfare of the most needy. Moreover, it is very clear that there is no altruistic aid. There is also the additional risk that aid could be evervating and could thus encourage the avoidance of hard decisions by recipients. There is no conclusive evidence for this, but common sense from routine observation reveals that the reaction of children, relatives, and friends toward frequent help is reduction, if not complete elimination, of independent effort. So also is it likely to be with countries depending heavily on aid.

In light of the preponderance of negative aspects of aid, the question then arises: Should aid be accepted or not? The answer will vary with interest groups. Those benefiting from aid on the recipient's side, such as policy makers, bureaucrats, and the local petty bourgeoisie, would argue that aid should be not only accepted but vigorously canvassed; and on the donor's side, especially the business, military, and political interests and the administrators of aid, there will be pressure for more aid. At the other extreme are those who hardly benefit from aid; these are the marginalized part of the population—the rural landless and subsistence farmers and the urban scum. They do not understand the adverse implications of aid and may reject it only on the ground that they are not benefiting from it—if they were, they would welcome it whether they understood the adverse implications or not. A middle position is occupied by a third group, composed of intellectuals, academicians, scholars, researchers, and a few perceptive government bureaucrats of integrity. This group has a clear understanding of the many negative aspects of aid, but some among them will accept it because it benefits them materially; some will totally reject it no matter what the consequences; and others will welcome it provided some conditions and limits are met. I belong to the third category. It is my position that aid should not be totally rejected but that care should be taken as to its conditions, type, and limits.

Let us take the example of a child. When it is born, it cannot sit; it cannot walk; it cannot even feed itself, an activity absolutely necessary for its survival. It is therefore gradually taught, over time, how to sit, walk, and feed on its own. As it advances in age, it is taught how to speak and to learn. Consequently, over the years, the child grows into a self-reliant man or woman. This self-reliance becomes possible only through the aid of people who are called either parents or guardians. Take yet another example, that of illness. No matter how strong one is, if one is taken seriously ill, one becomes bedridden and incapable of doing anything until aid comes from medicines and people—nurses and doctors in hospital and relatives at home. In this situation one becomes almost as a child. A third example, that of extreme old age, is similar. It is important to realize that aid is not all bad and that in fact in some cases it is necessary. What makes aid bad is the intentions behind it and the way it is utilized, because bad utilization fritters the aid away and excludes the needy from access to its benefits.

These examples show that aid should be accepted provided care is taken to control such things as the conditions (or strings), type, and limits. First, it is common knowledge that there is hardly any aid without strings, be they commercial, military, or political. Aid should be accepted with very minimal commercial strings but not at all with military or political strings. Commercial strings are just a diluted side of economic exchange. The reality is that even among industrialized countries, commercial exchange entails conflicts that are resolved through painful trade-offs and compromises. As for military and political strings, Europe, through the North Atlantic Treaty Organization (NATO), and Japan are under the economic and political control of the United States, just as Warsaw Pact countries are under the control of the Soviet Union. But there is a major difference where the LDCs are concerned. The NATO and Warsaw Pact countries and Japan have built sufficiently strong industrial capacity to afford them the political clout to resist successfully the hegemony of the United States and the Soviet Union, whereas the LDCs lack that power.

Second, care should be taken about the type of aid project: aid should be confined to technical assistance in training for technicians in various fields, in research, science, technology, and mathematics. In sum, the training should be in areas that will build or enhance the productive capacities of the recipients. There seems to be growing evidence that such aid is having a positive impact in Asia. On the other hand, aid in projects other than training tends to generate problems of maintenance for the simple reason that appropriate technical knowledge is lacking.

Third, care should be taken to set limits for aid. It should not just be poured into a country perpetually or even for a long time, otherwise it will be enervating and transform the recipient into a subservient country. The objective of aid should be to move the recipient as quickly as possible toward self-reliance. In this it is similar to the help given to a child or sick person, especially the latter, for as soon as the patients get well, they resume self-reliant activities. The fundamental thing to grasp here is that aid should be given within a specified period at the expiration of which it should be discontinued. Any continuation will prove enervating to the recipient and consequently defeat the objective of attaining self-reliance. This seems to be the threshold Tanzania is approaching, and it will be a violent contradiction with the country's strongly espoused principle of self-reliance.

The lessons for Africa are by now many and clear. African countries have had access to both experience and literature on aid and development, and therefore the time for decision is now, otherwise the danger of the aid trap is imminent. No development is ever wholly carried out on aid. Just as no person would develop his neighbor's home unless he could lay claim to it, so also no country will develop another one unless it will have substantial, if not absolute, control over it. After all, an OECD study reveals that development depends on factors other than aid—a leadership strongly committed to development, and a competent administration. Unfortunately, with respect to Africa the same study reveals the opposite attitude toward development: that of political resistance or indifference from a political leadership lacking commitment to the creation of a conducive environment for accelerating development.

7   Technology and Africa's Development

Technology is a vital tool of economic development. Its role in the economic development of the West has been amply documented, and today it is technology that Japan is using to surpass the United States in some areas of production, especially electronics and cars. What might be preventing Japan from engaging in space science is its costliness, the international politics involved, and perhaps its stand on war. Technology is also enabling two countries in Asia, China and India, to gain recognition and respect in global affairs. Their technologies may be crude relative to that of the West, but the most advanced technologically today started as crude and was refined over time. Similarly, Brazil occupies in Latin America the position China and India occupy among LDCs in Asia. Meantime, there is no single country in black Africa that has made any breakthrough, even in crude technology, for large-scale production. No North African country has attained any respectable level of technology, and no single African country could be described as partly developed or newly industrializing. The reason for all this backwardness is lack of advanced technology for processes and techniques of production. Africa is still far behind in long-range factors crucial to economic growth, namely education, technical and vocational training, and advanced scientific enquiry, which underpins advanced technology. Instead, Africa merely tries to import the results of scientific enquiry done somewhere else for use in a different cultural and socioeconomic environment. And what is called technology transfer is the importation of obsolete machinery from elsewhere by foreign firms for crude industrial production in African countries. Even in this case, Africans have two major handicaps. For the most part, they lack the specialized education to understand the scientific principles behind the operation of the machines, and where they do have the knowledge, they are not allowed access to machines or techniques.

Modern technology is crucial to growth, but Africa lacks it. Yet, after an exhaustive study of the history of the economic growth of West European countries over a long period of time, Simon Kuznets (1968) was led to the conclusion that technological revolution in agriculture is an indispensable base of modern economic growth. Given Kuznets's conclusion, which is supported by seemingly irrefutable evidence, Africa made a serious mistake in its development strategy because it neglected agriculture right from the beginning. Africa went straight for industrialization without building the base for it and for subsequent economic growth.

Again, Kuznets maintains that the industrialized nations have two major types of capital, knowledge and trained people. Africa lacks both in adequate quantity and quality except in a few areas that are not crucial to technological advance and high agricultural and industrial production. And even in cases where adequate knowledge exists in both quantity and quality, it is usually misused. Often highly trained people are placed in the wrong jobs or use much of their time doing administrative work instead of being able to do their professional work and thereby utilizing their specialized skills.

Two alternatives are open to Africa in order to acquire trained people, knowledge, and technology. One is, of course training. The other is adaptation. Training is easier, but expensive. However, Africa has been and is still pursuing this alternative to obtain trained manpower, knowledge, and some technical expertise. On the other hand, adaptation of knowledge and technology may be cheap, but there is no evidence that it is an easy thing to do. But it does seem that most people think it is easy to adapt, and perhaps this is one of the explanations for Africa's complacency with respect to technology. It seems adaptation is difficult for Africa in two ways. One is that it involves complex factors deriving from the cultural and physical environment; adaptation to the physical environment may be relatively easier, but adaptation to the cultural environment would be very difficult. Technology is supposed to be diffused, for it is meant to be used by the people to enhance productivity. Production is linked to culture, and unless technology is designed relatively simply enough and to fit the culture of the people, it will run the risk of being either not understood or being rejected outright, or both. That defeats the purpose.

The other way in which adaptation is difficult is explained by the rate at which technology is moving. In this respect one should distinguish between simple and sophisticated technology. The latter moves faster than the former because those who control technology need it more than they need simple technology, which is needed most by LDCs. But even simple technology moves relatively fast because of the desire on the part of private firms to make a profit. Therefore the issue is: Adaptation becomes extremely difficult not only because of the rapid changes in technology but also because of the variety spewed out. This problem will be discussed below in detail in the section on the technological gap. Meantime, suffice it to say that adaptation is not all that simple, and in addition it could discourage indigenous innovation.

Other important questions related to technology are its availability and diffusion. There is a tendency to conclude that technology is completely lacking for Africa's needs. This is true of sophisticated technology, but it is doubtful of simple or appropriate technology. Of course, technology is a dynamic thing and cannot be exhausted. Nonetheless, for the present needs of Africa, there seems to be enough. Appropriate technology is being poured into Africa both from foreign and from internal sources. There are profit-oriented firms and nonprofit organizations working on the technological needs of the LDCs that fit the cultural and socioeconomic environment. In Africa itself there are many research institutes engaged in many fields of technological application. In view of this, therefore, the problems of appropriate technology in Africa are the will to apply the available technology and its diffusion. In this chapter the argument is that appropriate technology is available for Africa, but much needs to be done to generate the will to apply it. When this happens, then greater efforts toward diffusion will be expected. Hence the main issue is the will to apply available technology.

However, another real problem of technology is the technological gap between Africa and the industrialized countries. The problem of closing such a yawning gap is daunting, but Africa requires to be innovative, otherwise it will continue to be dependent forever. Specific proposals are in the section on the technological gap below.

AVAILABILITY OF TECHNOLOGY

There is no doubt as to the availability of appropriate technology either for adaptation or for direct application, or for both. There are two pieces of fundamental evidence of the availability of technology in Africa, the number of international research institutions of which African countries are members, and the existence of local research institutions in many African countries. As of 1982, 26 African nations were members of the Current Agricultural Research Information Center. In addition, 30 were members of the International Information System for Agricultural Services and Technology. There are many other examples of local research institutions that are too numerous in Africa to enumerate, and more are being established.

But what is not clear is the impact of the existing institutions on the African socioeconomic environment. There is evidence that a substantial amount of output has been generated by these research institutes, but there is a big gap between this output and application. There does not seem to be a convincing explanation, except the lack of the will to apply it and the rapidity at which new technologies have been flooding the African market.

But before discussing examples of appropriate technologies available to Africa for direct application or adaptation, let us see what technology is. There are two definitions, but the one expounded by Harold Lasswell is preferrable. For a long time, technology has simply been defined as the application of science; in other words, it is the application of knowledge, for science in Greek means knowledge. On the other hand, Harold Lasswell defines technology as practices by which available resources are used to achieve valued ends. Both definitions are sound, but it seems that the difference is mainly in terms of sequence. There is no doubt that technology entails practices, that is, the handling of physical equipment to achieve certain ends, which, in turn, entails some form of output. In fact, most people understand technology more in its physical form or aspect than in any other form, hence the definition given by Lasswell is likely to appeal to more people than the definition that simply states that technology is the application of science. Though Lasswell's definition brings out more prominently the physical aspect of technology, it still retains the nonphysical aspect, and this is where the two definitions coincide. There are practices that are less physical than others. For example computer programs, also known as software, are constantly being developed, and they are ideas or symbols on paper that are fed into the computer to achieve some valued ends, mainly information output. But whatever the informational output, the fundamental thing is that the improvement in software is less of a physical object or activity. Similarly, the improvement of managerial or administrative practices may be the result of changes in communications systems, the designing of new rules, or the application of a model organizational structure, or some other similar change in some aspects of management or administration. This improvement is again less physical. Yet both examples could qualify as technological improvements. And this is where Lasswell's definition coincides with what one might call the classical one. What is common to both definitions is that they are characterized by some intensive mental activity, by some underlying scientific principles, by knowledge. So in technology, knowledge is the first stage, out of which come less tangible practices or physical objects that are used to produce valued outputs. There are cases, especially in LDCs, where gifted individuals could assemble contrivances that are useful for production. These may have been in existence for some time and, by the standards of the industrialized countries, be very crude. But the essence of my argument is that even if the technology is crude and the designer of the machine is ignorant of the principles behind its operation, those principles—that is, scientific knowledge—still exist. Those having advanced knowledge in the field concerned could easily identify the principles.

The foregoing analysis shows that defining technology is not easy, but suffice it to say that technology entails knowledge and principles that underpin the practices by which available resources are used or transformed to achieve valued ends. In many cases also, technology entails the construction of machines. But the populace perceives technology more in its physical form embodied in machines than its abstract form. This is the definition on which this discourse in based because the main interest here is appropriate technology, one that is simply designed and intended to help the majority but marginalized part of society in both the rural and urban areas of Africa.

Examples of technologies are drawn from three major sectors of the economy: agricultural and animal production, energy, and the surveying of resources. Several experts have eloquently analyzed new developments in technologies applicable to agriculture and animal production and to the surveying of resources by the use of satellites (*Ceres* Jan.-Feb. and Nov.-Dec., 1984). Therefore this discussion draws heavily from these sources.

The first major area of interest with respect to agricultural and animal production is biotechnology, or genetic engineering. This science has to do with the manipulation of genes. Genes are identified, isolated, removed, and transferred into cells of another organism of a different species, genus, or even kingdom. These cells then produce large numbers of clones genetically identical to one another (*Ceres,* Nov.-Dec., 1984). With this technology remarkable successes have been recorded in plant breeding, particularly in cassava and a variety of agricultural crops, especially rice. For instance, the International Institute of Tropical Agriculture in Ibadan, Nigeria, worked assiduously on cassava, starting with several thousand seedlings. Experiments and field trials reduced these to 100 clones. Further efforts and tests again brought the number to 20 and ultimately to the 5 best ones. Since then, the best clones have been distributed in Nigeria, Cameroon, Sierra Leone, Liberia, Zaire, Rwanda, and other African countries. The evidence is that they are doing well. This success has encouraged work on sweet potatoes in Cameroon.

Rice provides another good example of success in genetic engineering. As far back as 1977 a new variety of rice was produced in Pakistan with a maturity period of 20–25 days less than the local variety. This and other factors have combined to increase yield by 30 percent. In a similar way, rice and millet resistant to cold, disease, and downy mildew were developed in Hungary and India respectively. On the whole, in the area of plant breeding, more than 550 mutant cultivars of agricultural crops and ornamental plants have been produced, two-thirds of them through irradiation, another promising new technology.

Biotechnology, even by Western standards, is a breakthrough and sophisticated technology. The question then arises: In view of the sophistication of this technology, is it relevant to African needs? The answer is simply: Yes, it is. Africa's major crisis is a food shortage, and here are technologies that could be applied to raise food production quickly. This technology has a great potential for application in agriculture, where Africa's huge resources of labor and land are far from being utilized to the optimum level. However, there are threats that come from the rapidity at which technologies change and from profit-oriented corporations. Does Africa have the capacity to keep up with the rapid changes in technology and to compete with private corporations in their application? The fact is that, in both cases, Africa is at a great disadvantage. In the technological race LDCs, especially in Africa, are being left far behind. As to competing with private firms, it is significant that already about 50 corporations have been created in industrialized countries to exploit biotechnology.

But biotechnology is just one aspect of technological advance in agricultural and animal production. There are many other areas in which rapid technological progress is being made—for example, animal production, soil science, agro-chemicals, and insect and pest control, just to mention a few. In animal production ammoniated rice straw increased milk production by 50 percent in Sri Lanka. This would be a great boon to Africa, where, of the population of 380 million people in sub-Saharan Africa, around 40 million depend primarily on livestock production for their livelihood (*Appropriate Technology*, June 1986). Not only that, some 220 million (58 percent) of the population, in various ways and to varying degrees, depend on the productivity of animals.

In soil science many breakthroughs have been made. However, of special interest here is the discovery that only 30–50 percent of nitrogen fertilizer, when applied, is actually taken by the crop. The remainder constitutes a health hazard in the form of nitrate in drinking water. This revelation is of crucial importance to both Africa and fertilizer technology. For Africa the importance is in reviewing fertilizer policy all over the continent. Fertilizer manufacturers are obviously keen on dumping fertilizers on Africa, and in this they are supported by the conclusions of studies that maintain that one of the major constraints to African agricultural production is lack of adequate application of fertilizers. It is not being suggested here that fertilizers should be rejected but that alternatives to them as they are presently constituted should be found. This leads to another crucial aspect of fertilizer technology. In this regard, there is a need for efforts in research to reduce the harmful effect of fertilizers or even discover new sources of harmless fertilizers. In addition, it is well known that fertilizers, as they are presently constituted, are one of the factors that make modern agriculture very energy-intensive. A new technology that permits a new, less energy-intensive agriculture would be a boon to production as well as to environmental protection in this era of rapid depletion of resources and environmental destruction.

About insect and pest control there is no need to say much except that research is progressing well. There is no doubt that, in Africa, insects and pests are a major constraint to agricultural production.

What of the availability to Africa of technology in energy? In terms of appropriate technology, there are five sources of energy. These are animals, the sun, wind, forests, and agricultural residues. A sixth, geothermal energy, is being developed seriously mainly in Kenya and seems to be relatively expensive and hence inaccessible to the target group intended here, that is, the marginalized of society. For this reason it is not discussed here.

Animal power, like wind energy, has been in use for centuries, and so there is a tendency not to consider it as having anything to do with technology, especially when technology is perceived only in the sophisticated modern sense. Yet it is technology; in the sense Lasswell defines it as "practices by which available resources are applied to achieve valued ends," and the sense in which the contrivances and techniques by which animal power is used could be improved to extract more energy from the animal. Both the animals and the contrivances are resources.

Asia seems to make the best use of animals as a source of energy. Animals have been used for a long time there in post-harvest processing of crops and transportation: they are used for crushing sugarcane, threshing cereals, crushing oil seeds to extract oil, and transportation of people and produce to distant markets. The use of animals for ploughing is a well-known technology that does not need any elaboration. In Africa donkeys, cattle, and camels abound. Donkeys are used only as beasts of burden, but there have been attempts, still experimental, to use them for light plowing. Cattle have been used for plowing and for transportion; similarly, camels have mainly been used as beasts of burden, carrying people and produce over long distances. What is now needed is more research to diversify and improve the present level of this technology.

Experiments on solar energy have been going on in some parts of West Africa. Energy derived from this source is used for heating, drying, and cooking, but it is still far from being popularized, perhaps because of costs, other technological constraints, and the vested interests of multinational corporations that deal with conventional sources of energy.

Wind energy is used to drive a wind pump that is in production in Kenya. It is used for "pumping water for famine relief camps, livestock, crop irrigation, tree nurseries, clinics, and schools in five African countries." It "requires minimum of maintenance . . . and is designed to last more than 20 years, five times longer than a diesel pump" (*Small World,* Spring/Summer 1986). This is not a new technology. Wind pumps were used in Kano, Northern Nigeria, many years ago. However, there is every reason to expect some improvement in the performance of the latest wind pump. One would only hope that complacency on the part of African governments and the aggressiveness of diesel pump manufacturers and dealers do not obstruct the diffusion of this technology, which is of vital importance to rural production.

The energy derived from forests has become more efficient with the improvement of cooking stoves. This has a tremendous positive impact on both environment and rural production. And in fact, the impact on the environment has an indirect impact on production as well. At present, Africa's priority is not environmental considerations; it is production. The fast rate at which deserts are advancing is common knowledge. This is a consequence of denudation of vegetation arising from shifting cultivation, which is responsible for 70 percent of deforestation, overgrazing, and the gathering of fuel wood. There are no figures indicative of the rate at which overgrazing degrades the environment, but figures are available for fuel wood consumption. Wood accounts for 90–98 percent of energy consumption in rural areas, and nine out of ten people depend on it for energy. A combination of the effects of shifting cultivation and the use of wood as fuel accounts for the disapperance of forests at a rate of 0.6 percent a year. This is happening in most countries in Africa, and perhaps at a faster rate in the Sahel. How does this affect productivity? Vegetation cover provides organic fertilizers, conserves soil, and protects water courses. All these enhance production, and conversely, their destruction destroys production. Another way in which production is adversely affected is through the amount of time and energy spent in gathering fuel wood. As the population of both man and animals grows, two adverse consequences follow, competition between man and animals for the available vegetation cover and the growth in consumption of wood as fuel. As consumption grows, more and more trees are felled and forests recede, thus increasing the distance that has to be covered to obtain the wood for fuel. This increase in distance is responsible for the dissipation of time and energy that would have been saved for other productive activities. Concern for the tremendous rate of environmental destruction and wastage of resources in terms of time and energy has impelled the development of efficient stoves to conserve energy and hence wood. Energy-saving stoves are being developed and improved in several African countries such as Gambia, Sudan, Tanzania, and Zimbabwe. Improvement in efficiency is between 20 and 30 percent.

Agricultural residues, in addition to their use as livestock feed and in a variety of agro-industrial processing activities, can be sources of energy. This is a field associated with agro-chemical technology. There are two prominent examples: the fermentation of sugarcane waste to produce gas for use as fuel and the manufacture from coffee husks of briquettes for fuel. The latter has been developed recently in Kenya. These two energy sources could be of tremendous use to all coffee- and sugarcane-growing countries. Other possibilities exist: for instance, peanut shells, rice husks or straws, or some similar material could be transformed into bricks. But the constraint may be diffusion.

The above are just a few instances where appropriate technology could be made more available. There are other areas of interest that deserve attention, for example, post-harvest losses, food technology, and microcomputers.

Post-harvest technology is an area where African countries could be helped to eliminate hunger and save hundreds of dollars in foreign exchange that are spent on food imports. And what is needed, at this level of Africa's development, is not a sophisticated system of storage imported wholesale from somewhere else, for that would not fit Africa's socioeconomic and cultural environment. Therefore imported technology will of necessity require adaptation. But better still, technology in storage would only require the improvement of existing practices, which have been applied probably for thousands of years. In doing this, the repository of wisdom built over centuries by the farmers should be tapped: a technology developed in this way would meet the requirements of the socioeconomic and cultural environment.

A similar argument goes for food technology. African society, like other societies of the world, has had its indigenous foods since the beginning of agricultural practices. But later, modern contacts exposed African societies to exotic foods from other parts of the world and seduced Africans, especially the Westernized ones, to abandon their indigenous foods in preference to rice, wheat, and the like. And it happens that those who relish these exotic foods are the power elite whose policy of importing these foods has discouraged domestic agricultural production. This policy is being promoted despite the fact that Africa is very rich in food varieties. One ethnic group alone could boast of well over ten varieties of food. In an effort to promote indigenous foods, food technology institutions have been established and there has been success in at least a few recipes. A good example is that nonwheat flours of up to a proportion of 20 percent can be added to wheat flour to bake bread acceptable to consumers. In fact, recently the Federal Institute for Industrial Research in Oshodi, Nigeria, developed a bread made entirely from flours of local grains. It has been tested and found acceptable to consumers. The main problem is now diffusion: vested interests in wheat production and importation are fighting tooth and nail to prevent the popularization of this bread as a substitute. It is likely that this was the fate of locally derived food products developed by African research institutions elsewhere. In some cases, investors simply refused to adopt such products.

Microcomputers are being developed for use in the rural areas of Africa and are intended to be used for, among other things, medical diagnosis and agricultural and livestock production activities. This seems to be a neutral technology that does not have the constraints of socioeconomic and cultural environment except, perhaps, that of the availability of adequate and reliable statistical data. As to diffusion, it should have no problem because it is going to be applied by enlightened persons and there is no threat of competition from domestic technology.

Lastly, another useful technology available to Africa is satellite imagery, which is concerned with the survey of resources. It uses satellites to generate data by mapping resources and also gives warning about ecological as well as climatic conditions. Both functions are important for policymaking and developmental activities. A survey of resources provides data for development planning, and warning on ecological and climatic conditions gives policymakers the information and time required to plan for any impending disaster. There is no doubt that satellite imagery is a sophisticated technology, but it is also the type that is neutral to socioeconomic and cultural conditions. Hence Africa could use it without any problem of adaptation. In fact, the technology is not amenable to adaptation since it operates from space.

Europe and the United States have each developed a satellite for surveying resources and providing information on weather conditions and disasters. The European Meteosat, from a distance of 32,000 kilometers in space and in a single scene, covers all of Europe and Africa and much of the Near East and Latin America (*Ceres,* Nov.-Dec. 1984). Similarly, the United States has developed Landsat-5, which from a distance of 950 kilometers in space, can scan an area of 185 square kilometers in less than 30 seconds. It scans the globe once in every 16 days. While doing this it registers useful resources such as land and soils, pasture and range management, and water resources, forests, fish, and rural disasters such as heavy rainfall, desert locusts, flooding and flood damage, and weather conditions (ibid.).

It is clear that information on these items would be useful for policymaking and development planning in Africa. For instance, information on land resources and soils enhances policies and planning in agriculture, and that on water resources facilitates policies on and development of irrigation. With respect to water resources, the FAO is developing a drought watch over much of Africa that will alert governments to impending disaster and give them ample time to prepare for it. Similarly, data on pasture, range management, and forests are necessary for designing meaningful grazing and forestry management programs. This is useful not only in the efficient exploitation of resources but also in checking the alarming rate of desertification, which is the most serious disaster because it threatens Africa constantly with famine.

DIFFUSION OF TECHNOLOGY

The preceding discussion shows that the problem of technology in Africa is not that of availability. It may not even be that of adaptation. Africa has many research institutions working on a variety of appropriate technologies and moreover has access to many sources of technology that it could adapt. African nations are members of some important international research institutes through which they have access to technological information. There is also a large number of private firms and nonprofit organizations pouring out all sorts of intermediate technology. For these reasons, therefore, Africa's technological problems should be attributed to something other than availability. The problem is diffusion.

In the attempt to explain the problem of diffusion, attention was first concentrated on the attitudinal factor. In this respect, adopters of technology were categorized into three types: earlier adopters, who were considered risk takers, middle adopters, and laggards. But later, continuing research revealed that the problem of adoption can no longer be explained by attitude; it is now better explained by accessibility. It has now been established that African farmers, like any other farmers in other parts of the world, have a remarkable ability to adapt to new conditions and apply innovations.

But accessibility depends on affordability, which, in turn, hinges on resources. Those that have resources have access to the available technology, but such individuals are few compared with the mass of the farmers who need it most but have no means to get it. The problem of diffusion has now become something else: the problem of distributing the available technology among those who need it. There are three major aspects of the problem to consider: the level of the technology, that is, whether it is simple or sophisticated; the cost; and the participation of the beneficiaries in formulating and implementing technology programs.

The question of the level of technology has already been discussed above, and therefore here it is sufficient to reiterate two observations. First, at its present level of development, what Africa needs, especially with regard to rural production, is simple technology; and since technology, like the society it services, is dynamic, it will evolve into a more sophisticated one, over time, as the needs of the society demand. Second, there are a few technologies that are sophisticated, but also that Africa needs. Such technologies do not present problems of adaptation, for they are neutral as to the socioeconomic and cultural environment. They present only two major problems to Africa, namely control and cost. Sophisticated technologies are produced outside Africa; it is therefore natural that control remain at the source. But, in fact, Africa lacks the capability to operate and maintain machines that embody such technology.

Second, even simple appropriate technology proves inaccessible to the beneficiaries because of prohibitive costs. Technologies that are not affordable to those who need them most are irrelevant since they are not applied. Therefore one of the key solutions to adoption is reduction of cost.

Third, participation by beneficiaries is a fundamental aspect of the diffusion of technology because, like many other things, it is usually imposed on the beneficiaries. Policymakers and experts assume that they know better what the beneficaries want. But research has revealed that the people have a very clear perception of their felt needs. And to avoid irrelevance and the consequent waste of resources, this is where development efforts should start. The best way to do this is to give the beneficiaries the opportunity to participate in the planning and development of technology.

There are two aspects to participation in the development of technology, the sociocultural and the technical. The first aspect entails the participation of the populace at the grassroots level in determining their technological needs, and in planning and implementation of technological programs and projects. It also entails taking into account the cultural values of the beneficiaries because this ensures appropriateness, easy adoption, and relevance. Once these three conditions are met, irrelevance and waste will be avoided.

The technical aspect of participation has to do with installation and operation of the machines or equipment embodying the technology. Here the immediate problems of repair and maintenance and of the quality of the equipment usually arise. As to repair and maintenance, skills are almost completely lacking at the local level; with respect to quality, especially of equipment manufactured outside the users' environment, there is the problem that it wears out fast because of such factors as climate, unskilled handling, and lack of regular maintenance.

The above discussion of technology leads back to the conclusion that the fundamental problem of technology in Africa is that there is a general absence of firm and consistent policy. Then come the problems of accessibility and participation. But once policy is firm and consistent and long-lasting, other problems become relatively easier to solve, especially where adequate skilled manpower is available.

THE TECHNOLOGICAL GAP

The technological gap is the distance between African countries and the rest of the world with respect to technological knowledge and practices. It is an exogeneous factor impinging on the technological development of Africa. The technological race and mass production continually widen the gap. Africa has suddenly found itself with this extremely difficult challenge of the twentieth-century global environment. While Africa is struggling to avert famine, adequately feed its populations, and wipe out diseases such as malaria, yellow fever, and cholera, long forgotten elsewhere, others are going to space. The gap is unimaginable. So, what should Africa do? Should it content itself for the moment with intermediate technology, or should it boldly go for sophisticated technology with the aim of bridging the gap between itself and the rest of the world? Africa must do something, for technology is one of the most important answers to its production and health problems. It is technology that could save Africa from famine. It is technology that could save it from the scourge of disease. But bridging the technological gap in the near future is impossible.

Three institutions are involved in the generation of sophisticated technology: governments, private corporations, and nonprofit organizations. The first two have very close relations in the development of technology. Contracts flow from governments to corporations. For instance, in the United States corporations such as McDonnell Douglas and Boeing get contracts from the government to manufacture jet fighters and other war machines. In the Soviet Union and other socialist countries, the production of war machines, like other things, is the sole responsibility of wholly government-owned institutions. In capitalist countries the relations between government and nonprofit organizations is mainly that of tax exemption and perhaps a few regulatory conditions. In socialist countries, all major institutions are government owned, whether they are profit making or not.

Western governments have created institutions in a variety of fields in research and technology, the most important of which are space science and defense—the U.S. Pentagon is a clear testimony of this. However, governments are also involved in research and development in such areas as medicine, energy, engineering, chemistry, education, psychology, and the social sciences. Governments engage in areas that are unprofitable to private corporations or that may eventually be profitable but have long gestation periods. But in recent decades, space science has become one of the two most important preoccupations of governments in research and development. There is no need to discuss the reasons for government involvement and the research itself, it is sufficient and important to realize that space research is crucial to the defense and other industries of Western

Europe and the United States. In addition, some spin-offs of space research are applied in a variety of fields such as medicine and computer science.

Corporations are also major contributors to science and technology. That is precisely why they get government contracts to manufacture sophisticated war machines and other scientific equipment. Science and technology are crucial to the survival of these corporations in this world of fierce competition. Hence all corporations have research and development divisions or departments that keep them ahead, or at least abreast, of the latest technological developments. Failure to keep up means either loss of profit or extinction. The competition among corporations for survival and profit stimulates rapid advances in science and technology. Hence the rapidly yawning technological gap between Africa and, especially, Europe, the United States, and Japan.

Of the nonprofit organizations engaged in developing technology, some are privately owned, and some form a network of UN agencies. Though these institutions are neither profit making nor competing, they also make invaluable contributions to science and technology that are a reflection of the sheer dedication of all those associated with these agencies.

Since bridging the technological gap between Africa and the industrially advanced countries is impossible in the near future, the only feasible option for Africa, at present, is intermediate technology. It is more appropriate to African needs and is relatively easier and less expensive to develop. Nonetheless, it is still not easy to sustain the development of intermediate technology. There are three reasons for this difficulty. Competition, the first of these, has already been discussed. The second, pioneer status and the multiplier effect, are advantages in the technological race acquired by the industrially mature countries. These countries long ago laid the foundation of science and technology, a long lead that enhances the multiplier effect through spin-offs and other infrastructural advantages. These advantages Africa and other developing countries lack. And this multiplier effect is a very effective way of widening the technological gap between industrialized countries and the LDCs.

Mass production, the third aspect associated with competition, has a very adverse effect on the development of locally developed technology in Africa and elsewhere in the Third World. Whenever new appropriate technologies are developed, those who have the capability simply observe the new equipment and mass produce the same items but of superior quality, flood the market with them, and thus destroy local initiative. This problem is a real one and there are many examples of it. There is only one solution: the closing of African borders to new appropriate technologies from private sources and even UN agencies and nonprofit institutions, especially in countries where there is ongoing local initiative. The purpose should be to provide a challenge and thus compel countries to be innovative. However, cooperation with UN agencies and nonprofit organizations to develop technologies locally should not be disallowed. But even here, care must be taken to make sure that much of the initiative comes from local resources so as to build the capacity to sustain and maintain the technology after the withdrawal of the cooperators. The aim should be total autonomy to develop appropriate technology locally after a specified period of cooperation. But this aim cannot be attained without sealing the borders against a flood of externally developed appropriate technology that has already been initiated locally.

8 Conclusion: Challenge and Development

Europe . . . is the creation of the Third World.

Frantz Fanon

For all its strength, industrial civilisation had to be fed from without. It could not survive unless it integrated the rest of the world into the money system for its own benefit.

Alvin Toffler

But if African states all acted together, they could have some power at least to gravely inconvenience the Developed World.

Julius K. Nyerere

THE CHOICE

The struggle between the status quo and change will continue for a long time and will continue to assume a more violent form unless the privileged part of the world is ready to make some concessions. In this struggle to resist, Africa is the weakest of all continents. Nevertheless, it has a choice between acquiescence and freedom. Acquiescence is synonymous with dependence; freedom is synonymous with development.

The choice before Africa is clear: it is either development or dependency. However, one choice is easier than the other: the rational choice is the harder and the irrational one is the easier. The rational choice is to develop and hence throw off the shackles of dependency. The irrational choice is that of dependency, which guarantees perpetual underdevelopment. The two types of choice are discussed in greater detail below.

To choose the path of dependency is very easy but has dire consequences of a sociopolitical and economic nature. But it is easy only in the short run;

in the long run it is a very expensive venture. One may discuss the relative ease and costliness of choosing the path of dependency in terms of its internal and external dimensions. In its external dimension, it is relatively easy because it obtains support from those who have high stakes in the status quo, the industrialized countries of the world. The obvious local beneficiaries of such an easy path are the ruling elite. The external beneficiaries do two things to realize their objective: they corrupt the leadership of the dependent countries and back them with military force.

Corrupting the leadership of dependencies takes several forms, but two are outstanding, money and property. The ruling elite that has chosen the path of dependency usually holds accounts outside the country in which money may be deposited for it, and property is acquired for the leadership either in the home country or that of the external beneficiaries.

It is obvious that the path of dependency is not in the interest of the people. For this reason they are bound to resist it. On the other hand, the ruling elite and its paymasters in the metropolitan countries benefit from the existing relationship under which the populace is exploited. Hence the leaders maintain themselves in power through oppression and suppression, and in this, they get military support from their paymasters. This is the reason why some countries accept, when approached, military bases on their territory. Some even go to the extent of inviting industrial powers to establish such bases on their soil.

This leads to the costs of the internal dimension of dependency. As was mentioned earlier, the costs are both economic and sociopolitical. For practical reasons the two types of cost are inseparable, but it is useful to separate them for analytical purposes. Both are discussed in detail in the next section. Meantime, it is sufficient to note that there are two immediate internal costs of dependency, lack of political autonomy and sustained underdevelopment, which accounts for general poverty reflected in hunger, malnutrition, and disease. The lack of political autonomy is sustained not only by military force but also by blackmail: "Do this or we do that."

On the other hand, as I mentioned, the choice to develop is a hard one mainly because it entails both sacrifice and a fierce struggle against the status quo. They are both costs, albeit of different sorts.

It is doubtful whether any country, much less a continent, in this world as it is presently constituted will escape the influence of industrialism with its attendant materialism. Europe and North America have attained unprecedented levels of material progress with its attendant material welfare. For this reason, the problems of Europe and North America are no longer those of economic growth but of a type that economic growth as a remedy is unable to handle. The new problems are a reflection of the change in the structure of Western society. They reflect a conflict between material goods and what some scholars call positional goods. These problems are radically different from those prevailing in Africa and hence require solutions other than mere economic growth. While North America and Europe are grappling with social problems that are mainly not of a material nature, Africa is preoccupied with war against poverty. As a solution to its problems, Africa needs material progress and hence economic growth, and in the shortest possible time. Ralf Dahrendorf (1981) aptly summarizes the African dilemma as a case of "trying a jump in development combining poverty with equity and political participation simultaneously." This is a formidable task but one that must be accomplished if Africa is to take its place in the comity of continents.

This brings us to the question of sacrifice. Africa, like other Third World continents, is aiming at a jump in development, a jump that entails many hardships, the most obvious of which are strains and stresses and sacrifice. The acquisition of anything, material and nonmaterial, involves a trade-off, which, in the case of development, is sacrifice. Development is a long-term task, and it needs investment today for the sake of the future. This is where the sacrifice comes in. Africa is materially poor because of a combination of the effects of parasitism by advanced societies and its lack of capacity to exploit its own resources. Yet, amid this poverty, Africa has to set aside some "surplus" for investment if it is to develop. This is the hard sacrifice.

Then there is the problem of the forces of status quo. The dependency relationship was established long ago and has existed since the days of colonialism and imperialism. It prevails to this day in a slightly modified form known as neocolonialism, so called because it is less direct but its objectives and the effects on dependent countries remain the same. Among the objectives are the continuance of the existing high material standards of living in the industrialized countries, their high levels of employment—in the words of Toffler (1980), "jobs of millions of ordinary workers came to depend on it" (neo-colonialism)—and their military strength, which is a tool for maintaining the status quo. The effects of the realization of these objectives on Africa are the absence of political autonomy, and exploitation and its attendant adverse consequences, which have been mentioned above. It is the effort to maintain this inequitable relationship and the benefits derived from it that unleash the forces of the status quo against the struggle to develop. Hence the prevalent political instabilities in the Third World.

In the light of what has been discussed above, what choice has Africa made? In terms of rhetoric, especially in recent years when it has been experiencing sustained economic crises, Africa has chosen the path of development. Many resolutions, at both regional and global levels, have been made by African countries, but they are hardly accompanied by commensurate resources and actions. Consequently, the resolutions remain merely paper ones. Any talk about development in Africa is rhetoric until it is accompanied by a commensurate amount of resources and action. This means that, in reality, Africa is as steeped in dependency as ever before. Nothing reveals this more than Africa's helplessness in the face of the prevailing global economic turbulence. For this reason it is necessary to examine in detail the adverse consequences of dependency for Africa.

THE CONSEQUENCES OF DEPENDENCY

The consequences of dependency for Africa are of two broads types, economic and political. Some of the economic consequences have been referred to above, and therefore only a few examples will be discussed here.

The root of African dependency is colonialism; before its advent, African economies were relatively self-sufficient and closed. Of course, disruption started with the slave trade, which for centuries preceded colonialism. The slave trade took its toll of the African labor force, causing loss of production to Africa and a corresponding gain in production for the British, the Portuguese, the Spaniards, the French, and the North American colonialists, just to mention a few. Despite the ravages to the black African economies occasioned by the slave trade, much of their structure and mode of production survived, only to be penetrated and diluted. If the structure and mode of production had been left to develop autochthonously, perhaps the story for Africa would have been different today. It is probable that Africa would have been at a much higher level of material development than it is today, whether it chose the capitalist or the socialist path of development. If it chose the capitalist path, it would have autonomously developed the bourgeois class necessary for capital accumulation. But alas for Africa, this chance was violently thwarted by colonialism and its successor, neocolonialism.

The fundamental and immediate objective of colonialism was exploitation for reasons that are common knowledge. The one thing that facilitates exploitation is the opening of an economy. This is the only way of incorporating an economy into the world capitalist system, for the system depends heavily on such incorporation. This explains the instability that the economies of the Third World, especially in Africa, suffer. Openness has a positive correlation with the global economic instability. The greater the openness, the greater the intensity of the instability. The degree of openness varies with countries. In most cases, small countries and those with monocultural economies are prone to openness and hence are vulnerable to global economic instability. On the other hand, larger countries are in a better position to close their economies and thus insulate themselves; India and China are good examples. China is purported to have opened its economy recently to the global economic system, but it is still doubtful whether foreign trade constitutes any significant proportion of its GDP. As for India, at least between 1961 and 1976, the economy was relatively closed. During this period, the share of the external sector in the national income hovered around an average of 5 percent. There is hardly any doubt that this is one of the fundamental reasons for the relative development and autonomy of the Indian economy.

But the story is different with large countries such as Argentina, Brazil, Mexico, and Nigeria. Of the four, Brazil is relatively more advanced industrially but at a high cost because of the openness of its economy. Despite being relatively advanced industrially, which puts it among the NICs, Brazil is at present grappling with two major problems. The more publicized is its debt burden: along with Argentina and Mexico, it is one of the three most indebted countries in Latin America and hence the developing world. The second is that evidence has been accumulated by economists to the effect that ordinary Brazilians are not partaking of the benefits of Brazil's rapid economic growth over the last two decades. It is probable that Brazil's economy is controlled from outside, especially by the United States. Argentina and Mexico, if anything, are in a worse economic situation. Both are relatively less industrialized and have less ability to meet their debt obligations than Brazil. The explanation of this is too much openness.

Nigeria's case is worse still, and it is in a much weaker position. Nigeria is as open as Argentina and Mexico, if not more so, and in addition it is relatively much less industrialized. The prevailing global economic recession, which started around 1981, has for the first time exposed the bankruptcy of the Nigerian economy. It was suddenly discovered that Nigerian industry is heavily import-dependent. Consequently, 60 percent of its industries use imported material constituting up to 80 percent of the industrial output. Nothing has exposed Nigeria's weakness and dependency more than this.

Though some large countries have failed to use the advantage of their size to close their economies and develop, it seems small countries are far more vulnerable to openness and its adverse consequences. This is especially true of countries that depend heavily on a single or very few agricultural crops to earn foreign exchange. A few examples from other parts of the world are appropriate.

From 1971 to 1975, Guatemala depended on coffee, bananas, cotton, and sugar for 55 percent of its total exports. The situation seems worse in El Salvador, which depends on coffee, cotton, and sugar for 64 percent of its total exports, while 90 percent of its exports go outside the Central American Common Market.

In Asia, Malaysia, Singapore, Taiwan, Hong Kong, and South Korea are good examples of openness and dependency. For Malaysia, indicators of the degree of openness are available. For instance, from 1971 to 1975 rubber, tin, saw logs, petroleum, and palm oil formed 70 percent of exports. In the same period the value of rubber exports constituted 40 percent of exports. In sum, the degree of openness is reflected in the fact that the foreign trade sector accounted for 40–50 percent of the GNP. Though I do not have indicators of openness for the other Asian countries mentioned, it is well known that they are all appendages of Western capital, and that is why they are hailed as models of growth and development. It is common knowledge that Taiwan and South Korea are U.S. economies, and for historical reasons one would expect Britain to be the dominant force in Hong Kong and Singapore, with some inroads by some European countries.

Because of the benefits they get from the openness and dependency of the Third World economies, the industrialized countries extol the virtues of free trade, but at the same time protectionism has been increasing in recent years. As of now, 11 countries have the potential to join South Korea, Hong Kong, Brazil, Mexico, Singapore, and Taiwan as NICs. They are bound to capture a proportion of the market controlled by the industrialized countries, hence the rising protectionism. This is an attempt to keep these countries in their dependent role. Free trade is the single most important benefit of openness; it is the engine of growth in the open economies. But while these countries are growing economically, the markets for their exports are being closed.

Dependency is a very weak position, as illustrated in the following statistics: As far back as the mid-1970s it was estimated that a rise of 1 percentage point in growth in industrialized countries induces 0.5 percent and more than 1 percent short- and long-run growth rates, respectively, in LDCs. Conversely, a 1 percent increase in the growth rate of LDCs as a whole induces only 0.08 percent rise in the growth rate of industrialized countries. In addition, in the global monetary system designed and controlled by Western Europe, the United States, and Japan, LDCs have no influence whatsoever. Yet this is the most powerful engine of growth and trade in the global system. No wonder it is the most effective tool used to keep developing countries in subservience.

In Africa, openness is well aided by faulty economic policies and bad economic management in increasing and sustaining dependency. Bad choice of economic policies has already been discussed in chapter 3; bad economic management is analyzed later in this chapter under the heading "Challenge and Development." They are, however, touched on here because they relate to the political consequences of dependency.

The second consequence of dependency is the political cost, which is reflected in the general discontent of the society. This discontent arises from faulty economic policies and mismanagement and is a reflection of poor leadership that is not committed to development.

Wrong economic policies have been touched on earlier. They are policies that promote an economic development strategy that is not rooted in the needs of the populace. Such a development strategy is usually outwardly oriented to meet the needs of the metropolitan countries. Internally, it meets the needs of the ruling elite, needs that are very different from those of the populace. Whereas the needs of the populace are the basic necessities of life, those of the metropolitan countries are raw materials, and those of the ruling elite are luxury goods.

Meanwhile, with faulty economic policies goes economic mismanagement. Mismanagement takes several forms, but first it starts with the wrong policies, which deploy resources to areas of production least useful to the populace. While such resources are used to produce luxury goods for the urban populations, especially the power elite, rural production suffers, the consequence of which is lower output, income, employment, and hence intolerably poor living conditions in the rural areas.

One other aspect of mismanagement is corruption. The two are closely associated. Corruption finds vent in so-called development projects, which entail a multitude of activities ranging from the acquisition of land through importation of materials, machinery and equipment and construction. These activities usually necessitate the use of contractors. At every stage of the project from the initial feasibility studies to actual execution, two types of interests meet: those of the political-bureaucratic elite on the one hand and those of the contractors on the other. The symbiotic relationship established between the two interest groups involves the exchange of money. For awarding and signing the contract, the political bureaucratic elite gets its percentage kickback; lower-echelon civil servants get their own share as formalities leading to the physical execution of the project proceed. This phenomenon explains the preference for big projects by the top political-bureaucratic elite and the desire to have as many projects in the pipeline as possible, even if the capacity to implement them is conspicuously lacking.

The reason for emphasizing the problems of bad development policies and economic management is their close association with political instability. The populace cannot continue forever watching the power elite alone enjoy the benefits of economic progress. Therefore, they react, especially in times of economic hardship. When the economy is functioning "well," even in a very exploitive framework, the chances of reaction are not very high except in a fairly educated and sophisticated society. But in times of economic hardship, even the most ignorant population reacts in one way or another. Such reactions are especially violent where IMF prescriptions are being applied to "revive" the economy. The degree of reaction varies with countries and the openness or otherwise of the government. However, whatever the difference, the fact remains the political upheavals or instabilities constitute a cost of dependency.

INTERDEPENDENCE

The Third World economy is collectively a dependent economy. Yet it is a mistake to think that the Third World alone is dependent: the truth is that the industrialized nations are also dependent. This means that both worlds are dependent—on each other. But this should not detract from the fact that the relations are very unequal. The relative positions of dependence differ markedly; the gap is huge. Undoubtedly, the Third World is the weaker of the partners, for many reasons, such as too open and very weak economies arising from exploitation by the advanced industrialized countries; lack of science and technology and hence weak productive capacity; and the absolute absence of strong military backing. The weak position of the Third World is reflected in its inability to absorb external shocks generated by global economic recession.

On the other hand, the industrialized world is very strong. Its economy is very strong, it has science and technology, the most important engines of progress, and it is backed by a very powerful military machine. All these confer autonomy on its economy and society. Its economy, individually and collectively, is so strong that it easily absorbs any global economic recession, however severe. In fact, global economic recession is generated by changes not in the economies of the Third World countries but in those of the industrialized countries. Yet, with all this economic, industrial, and military might, for the raw materials and strategic minerals that feed the industrial, technological, and military machines of the industrialized nations, they are heavily dependent on the Third World. Some examples of this dependence are necessary: they are given at both the global and the country level.

At the global level, estimates in the early 1970s revealed that the Third World produced nearly all of the world's coffee, cocoa, beans, bananas, palm kernel, jute, and natural rubber; more than 70 percent of tea, peanuts, and timber; and nearly 60 percent of rice and 40 percent of cotton. Now, in the 1980s, there is no evidence that the dependence of the industrialized countries on the Third World for these raw materials has declined. During the same period, the heavy dependence of the West on the Third World countries for energy was exposed by the increase in the prices of crude petroleum in 1973. Though this development intensified research into alternative sources of energy, it has as yet to have much impact in lessening the dependence of the West on petroleum.

At the country level, a good example is the U.S. dependence on petroleum oil, the bulk of which it obtains from the Middle East. This heavy dependence was exposed during the oil embargo of 1973. The U.S. reaction was very strong and was directed not at the principle of the embargo itself, but rather at the fact of its heavy dependence on the Middle East. As a reflection of this dependence, the United States, through its secretary of state, Henry Kissinger, issued a threat that it would resort to force if necessary to keep the Middle East oil flowing to the United States. In addition, the U.S. secretary of energy recently called on its European allies to build strategic stocks of oil with the aim of bringing down oil prices in the future. And in another development, President Reagan has had the occasion, following the escalation of the Iran-Iraq war, to say that the United States was very much interested in new developments in the war and to add that the flow of oil to the United States must be maintained. This is a veiled threat to use force, should the need arise.

With respect to strategic minerals, the United States exhibits similar dependence. The Department of Defense requires 62 strategic materials of critical importance for its programs. For 52 of these, it depends on foreign countries, and three-quarters of these materials come from the Third World. In addition, the nuclear industry is dependent on strategic minerals found mainly in Africa.

If the vast and rich United States depends so much for its supplies of oil and strategic minerals on the Third World, the similar heavy dependence of other industrialized countries is a foregone conclusion. In this respect, Japan is the most vulnerable, and examples have been mentioned in chapter 1. It is obvious that Europe and North America are heavily dependent on the Third World for their energy and strategic minerals needs; their industrial machines cannot function without ample supplies from the Third World. But this dependence notwithstanding, why is it that industrialized Europe, North America, and Japan maintain their superiority in their relations with the Third World? There are four major reasons: science and technology, finance capital, the high proportion of trade among themselves, and the backing of a powerful military machine.

It has already been mentioned that science and technology are one of the most important tools of economic progress possessed by the West. The two inseparable tools of economic progress are the two things that the West has given the modern world and that have raised the material condition of humanity probably to an unprecedented level. The use of the word *probably* may be surprising, but there is reason for it. There is no doubt that our world of today has attained a very high degree of scientific and technological development, yet scholars and researchers concerned with the origins of civilization have been accumulating evidence that tends to lead to the conclusion that far superior civilizations created by some far superior beings preceded our present one. Surely, the evidence is still far from conclusive, but at the same time it is very difficult to ignore what has been collected so far.

The digression notwithstanding, the fact remains that the West is the pioneer in modern science and technology, a status that confers on it the monopoly of the tools of economic development. These tools are the foundations of industrialization and hence the basis of their economic power. Other countries of the world have been busy for generations and are still busy trying to obtain these two "secrets," and yet the gap remains wide. Among the LDCs, only China and India have any early propects of breakthrough. Israel has the capability, but it might be constrained by finance. The cost of nuclear and space programs is staggering. And as to other developing countries, especially those of Africa, the technological gap is widening. The problem is not only finance; more serious is the absence of capability in terms of manpower with the necessary skills.

The second reason for the paradox of European-U.S. dominance over and dependence on the global system is capital. There are two types of capital: capital stock—constituted of machinery, equipment, and technology—and finance capital. In both, the West has a monopoly because of its advantages as a pioneer. Machinery and equipment are derived from science and technology, in which the West has unquestionable superiority. Stock of physical capital is another indispensable tool of economic progress, and for this reason the developing countries clamor to get it along with technology. And at first, the only source of physical capital and technology was the West. Now other sources are available, but the West still remains the sole source of sophisticated machinery and technology and the dominant source of "ordinary" machinery and the technology embodied therein. The latter is the type of capital the Third World struggles to obtain from the West with its hard-earned foreign exchange.

Then there is the more ubiquitous financial capital, the lubricant of the capitalist machine. Europe and the United States are capitalist, and the driving force of capitalism is profit, which is obtained from the investment of capital used to purchase labor, machinery and equipment, and materials. Capital is also exported to other countries where the prospects for making huge profits are much higher than in the home country.

Trade is another fundamental aspect of capitalism, which cannot survive without a tremendous volume of exchange at the global level. It is capital (money) that mediates this flow of exchange. There is more exchange where there is more production and consumption. There is more production and consumption, and therefore more exchange, in Europe, North America, and Japan than anywhere else. Hence the greater need for finance capital.

So for reasons of profit, trade, production, and exchange, finance capital is of tremendous importance to the West. It was in recognition of this importance that, as far back as 1941, the United States began planning the financial strategies for the postwar reincorporation of the peripheral as well as other economies of the world into its control, hence the establishment of institutions such as the World Bank and the IMF. Consequently, the United States dominated the world system from 1944 until the early 1970s, when its hegemony was seriously challenged.

The financial system of the world is unquestionably controlled by the West, which uses this power to control the Third World in two fundamental ways, through the LDCs' dire need of capital for development and by being an outlet for "investment" by the rich of the Third World. Developing countries need finance capital to purchase physical capital and materials for development, and they also need money (capital) to purchase even consumer goods and services. And they obtain this capital through exports and through loans, grants, and other forms of aid. The disadvantages of aid have been discussed above. Suffice it to repeat here that aid is one source of subservience. Another, which has become topical recently, is debt. Many LDCs have been induced to overborrow and are now facing the embarrassing consequences. This development has effectively put the borrower countries under the control of the lenders to the extent of enabling the latter to meddle with the former's internal affairs.

Meanwhile, the West, as an opportunity for investing financial capital, offers two alternatives. It takes two forms and it comes from two sources. One form of investment is putting the money in various types of deposits; another is the purchase of property or stocks and shares, where the host country allows. One source is governments, the other individuals. The sources are of more interest here.

Governments can and do invest their excess liquid funds in the West, a type of investment that started during the colonial period. As far as I know, Britain compelled its colonies to invest their surplus funds in the metropolis. Whether it was the case with colonies under other countries, I do not know. Today independent governments are investing their money in Europe and the United States. These governments are those of the petroleum-exporting countries of the Middle East, which, from the late 1960s to the mid-1970s, accumulated a lot of foreign reserves that their economies could not absorb and that they could not allow to remain idle. Therefore, the only alternative was to invest the reserves, and the only outlets were Europe and the United States.

Individuals who invest are usually members of the political-bureaucratic ruling elite and monarchs and their families. Both types of rulers maintain secret accounts in Switzerland and other European countries as well as in the United States and also acquire properties. This is true of most African and Middle Eastern political leaders. However, in the case of monarchs and their families, there is the peculiar problem of separating the property of their governments from their own. For this reason, investments by governments of the Middle East should be interpreted with care. The case of the late Shah of Iran provides one example of what may be happening there. When the Shah died, he left property and other assets valued at some billions of dollars in the United States that later became a bone of contention between the revolutionary government of Iran and the United States. Nonetheless, the underpinning argument is that the Shah, lacking any business concern of the size of, for instance, General Motors, was unlikely to own assets of such magnitude from any source other than government, if the monarch is at all separable from government. And the inseparability of the monarch from the government is a characteristic of all monarchical systems, of which there are several oil-rich examples in the Middle East.

The third explanation of Western power is trade. This lies not necessarily in the volume of trade, but in the direction. It is true that the West buys much of the industrial raw materials it needs from the Third World, but the subsequent trade in manufactured goods is conducted more within the West itself. For instance, in 1960, two-thirds of the import trade of industrialized countries was constituted of goods exchanged among themselves, a proportion that rose to three-quarters in 1971. There is as yet no evidence that the proportion has decreased since then. This fact clearly shows that the West has less need of the Third World as far as trade in manufactured goods is concerned. But conversely, because of dependence, the Third World has more need of the West in trade both in raw materials and in manufactured goods. Eighty percent of the trade of the former is done with the latter.

The fourth and last explanation of Western power is the backing of its powerful military machine, which is used both to bend the will of intransigent countries that are struggling to attain or defend their independence and in the ideological cold war with the socialist bloc. A good example is the U.S. involvement in Nicaragua, El Salvador, and other Latin American countries. In Africa, the United States of America is in South Africa, Angola, and the Sahrawi Democratic Republic, to mention a few instances. Similarly, several U.S. threats of military intervention in the Middle East to keep oil flowing should be recalled. Yet such threats by the United States are not confined to the Third World. West Germany and Japan are heavily dependent on the military power of the United States, and it is even prepared to use nuclear arms as a last resort in order to keep Japan and Western Europe within its sphere of influence.

CHALLENGE AND DEVELOPMENT

Africa has been in economic crisis for more than a decade, and this crisis has been attributed to a variety of factors both historical and recent. Historically, colonialism was at the root of the problem, and wrong policies aggravated the situation. At independence, African leaders inherited colonial economic structures that were designed for the benefit of the colonial master. The first priority of African leaders should have been to change the economic structures they inherited for the benefit of their peoples. Development strategies should have been rooted in the people right from the outset. Unfortunately, a mistake was made, whether out of ignorance or deliberately: the wrong development strategies were imbibed, and policies were elitist and outward-looking. Agriculture was neglected, and the basic needs of the people were ignored after a few years of effort to provide people with social services. Nothing was done about raising the productive capacity of the people or the economy. Instead, the production of raw materials for the industries of the West was stepped up. Africa was indoctrinated with the fetish of foreign exchange, and so all production beyond subsistence was geared toward earning it. This mode of production continued until population growth overtook the archaic production structures inherited from colonial times.

There is no doubt that external factors such as colonialism and the recent so-called global recession have contributed to the economic distress of Africa. But from the outset, I have argued that internal factors, especially in recent years, have contributed more to the problem than the external ones. Now, after a quarter of a century of independence, African countries have little excuse for blaming global economic recession, much less colonialism, for their economic problems. True, African economies are open and hence cannot be completely insulated from global economic dynamics, but a sufficiently long time has elapsed to enable these countries to take steps to minimize the impact of external economic changes. They could have done this by restructuring their economies and adopting the correct development policies and strategies; they should have taken steps to root their development policies and strategies in the people and to reduce their dependence on industrialized countries by promoting greater exchange among themselves. In taking these steps to reduce their dependence, African nations would surely have been inundated with theories spelling inevitable doom for such strategies. The best way to deal with this problem is to ignore the prophets of doom completely; any attempt to listen to them is a recipe for failure.

Africa has adopted solutions offered by the conventional wisdom to resolve the economic crisis, but these have failed, for two simple reasons: first, they do not address the root of the problem, namely the structure of the African economies; and second, instead they promote openness and greater dependency through the intensification of efforts to produce more agricultural raw materials and mining more minerals.

Following the failure of solutions offered by conventional wisdom, it is encouraging that African countries are beginning to realize the need for a new development strategy, even if only at the level of rhetoric. Consequently, the OAU has started reorienting itself away from political and toward economic issues. Though political issues are not neglected, economic ones have started attracting greater attention in recent years: there has been more talk about regional cooperation, agriculture and rural development, and self-reliance. Translating the talk into action is very difficult, but the recognition of the need for change itself is a good starting point.

Africa is still in the course of formulating concrete agricultural and rural development strategies. However, one crucial area of development, technology, is hardly mentioned. It is true that pockets of technological policy exist in some countries, but it seems these are few. What is required is for each African nation to have a coherent technological policy, and for these to be coordinated and formulated into a regional policy.

To recognize the need for change in development strategy is one thing; to act on it is another. Development is a challenging and long-term business. The fundamental development challenge to Africa is environmental, by which I mean the global community, especially of Europe and North America. These parts of the world have attained very high levels of material development; they are said to have "arrived" at the peak of material culture and to have become a model for the rest of the world. Africa is one of those regions struggling to emulate the West, but it faces two major constraints. First, Africa has to close the development gap between it and the West in the shortest possible time. Second, while it is trying to do so, the technological gap is widening. These are formidable challenges that call for hard thinking, innovation, and hard work. The challenge Africa is facing is far harder than the one the West faced in the course of its development. Europe and North America developed in a world that was scientifically and technologically underdeveloped and did not face the challenge of a more developed world than themselves. So they developed at their own pace, and that pace was slow and painful. Africa does not have the luxury of developing at a leisurely pace, for it is struggling to develop in the space age. The dynamics of change in science and technology are simply tremendous.

Another constraint to Africa's development is the handling of policy and management. Together with the global environment and the style of politics in Africa, this problem explains, perhaps more than anything else except absence of political will, the failure of development efforts in Africa. There are three major problems in the handling of policy and management: political infighting, weak policy formulation, and a high "mortality" rate of policies. Political infighting, which was touched on earlier, has to do with the struggle for power among different political parties in a multiparty system and among factions within the same party in a single-party state. Of interest here is how such infighting obstructs the formulation and implementation of policy. It does this in a simple way: those committed to a struggle for power cannot have time to draw up sound policies for development. They commit scarce resources, including time, to the fight for power, a colossal waste indeed, which would be interesting for social science researchers to explore. It is likely that their research would reveal staggering instances of waste. But even if the waste does not turn out to be colossal, it may be sufficiently substantial as to be a cause for concern.

The other problem of policy is that of weak formulation, that is, the weak base on which it is formulated. There are two explanations for the formulation of weak policies. The first is, of course, the struggle for power among the elite. People struggle for power not so much for its own sake as for the privileges it confers on whoever has it. Few people struggle for power just for its own sake, and perhaps fewer still in order to apply it to the benefit of the people. Both assertions seem to be universally true: they seem to be true even in the industrially advanced countries. However, one major difference between developed and developing countries is that there is less incidence of the abuse of power in the former than in the latter, and where it does occur, it is subtle. The reasons are probably that the societies of the industrialized countries are educated, and hence have a fair knowledge of their rights, and that they are politically conscious. This compels accountability on the part of those in power. Nevertheless, the basic argument here is that in the LDCs, where the struggle for power is fierce because of the privileges it confers and where the incidence of abuse is greater, members of the power elite have no time for or commitment to sound policy formulation and implementation. Another explanation of weak policies is a weak statistical or information base because of the inadequacy of the available statistics or information needed for the formulation of sound policies. But even where reliable statistics or information is available, for example, about the modern sector, a fundamental problem arises: policymakers may not be interested in using available information to formulate policies but may prefer to allow themselves to be guided by political calculations. And even where the policymakers do use available information, the success of the policies is usually hampered by the high degree of uncertainty in the environment.

The third problem of policy in Africa is what one may call the high mortality rate. The policy environment is highly volatile: policies are changed at such a frequent rate as to attain a breathtaking speed in some countries. Extremely few, if any, African countries are endowed with the tenacity of purpose to maintain the same policies for a reasonably long time. It is not being advocated here that policies should not change, but rather that they should be changed at a reasonable pace and on reasonable grounds. Policies must change, because society is dynamic and they are designed for the benefit of society. Nonetheless, they should be allowed to take root and their effectiveness and success assessed over a reasonable period of time, and then they should be changed only when the need arises. But that is not the case in Africa. First, policies are formulated hurriedly and on weak bases for reasons already examined, and this, of course, is one of the main explanations of the high mortality rate. Obviously, hurriedly contrived policies can hardly survive even in a stable socioeconomic environment, let alone a turbulent one such as Africa's. Second, Africa seems to be a victim of a deluge of ideas. All manner of consultants, researchers, scholars, and experts bombard it with ideas or "new" and "more viable" strategies and programs. And Africa is very gullible in succumbing to this army of wizards of development. But the problem is not lack of ideas, or strategies, or programs, or projects; it is the lack of the will to achieve and of the tenacity of purpose. Africa lacks even a clear vision of what it wants to do and where it is going. Perhaps this is the main explanation of Africa's gullibility to the so-called new ideas, which are in fact more of the same thing. There are other possible explanations: the desire to develop fast and corruption, for example. Where there is desire to develop, it is highly unlikely to be development that is for the benefit of the masses; it is development that ministers to the needs of the elite. In the case of corruption, the strategy is that new ideas generate new and many projects from the formulation, design, and implementation of which the political-bureaucratic establishment benefits. This phenomenon was analyzed in chapter 7.

   I have all along been discussing the problem of policy. But as I noted earlier, Africa's policy problem has its twin brother, management. Surely, the two are closely interrelated: policy supplies management with projects to execute. Management's problems have to do with both policy and resources. The activities of management or administration are justified by policy: policy tells it what to do. But as I pointed out above, policy has major problems, namely rapid change and the inevitability of operating in an environment of great uncertainty, in some cases to the level of volatility. Administration shares both problems. An additional one for management in the Africa environment is, of course, that of reliable statistics or information, but this is less serious. The first two problems have to do with guidance, but because of rapid change in policies, guidance is not properly forthcoming. Consequently, management is also subject to sudden change of direction. Hence chaos. In terms of resources my view is that the main problem is poor utilization and wastage rather than scarcity. Scarcity exists, but it is intensified by wastage as manifest by misutilization of manpower and bloated bureaucracies.

   I now return to the question of what Africa should do in the challenging environment in which it has to develop. There is one main answer: Unite.

There is simply no alternative. The best-known exponent of this strategy so far is Mwalimu Nyerere, ex-president of Tanzania and chairman of the OAU in 1984–85. Unity is so important in Africa's development strategy that it deserves detailed analysis. The analysis here is based on Ali Mazrui's concepts of organic and strategic solidarity. Mazrui applies these notions to the Third World as a whole, including Africa. But first, what is meant by organic and strategic solidarity?

Mazrui defines organic solidarity as greater economic integration among Third World economies and strategic solidarity as a decrease in the South's dependence on the economies of the North. Africa needs both strategies, and the second must be underpinned by the first, otherwise dependence cannot be decreased. There must be economic integration before there can be any hope of success in reducing dependence. Economic integration is a form of unity—economic unity. And the importance of unity for strategic solidarity lies in the fact that the North is ever ready to neutralize any efforts at unity made by the South.

Mazrui identified three main differences between the North and the South: technology (rather than income), efficient organization, and skill (rather than income or numbers). There is no doubt that skill is the linchpin of both technology and organization, and this has been recognized by Africa, even if dimly, but again the problem is action.

Surely, African countries train their citizens in various skills, but the problem comes when the training is either inadequate or in irrelevant fields. However, one common problem of Africa seems to be that the politicians or power elite are averse to using local experts, perhaps because of mistrust, perhaps because of corruption. The average African politician always mistrusts a local expert. And what is baffling is that even the educated politician succumbs to this paranoia. Mistrust by a semiliterate or relatively less-educated politician is understandable: the reason is an inferiority complex and some perceived "threat" to his privileged position. Yet the perceived threat is just an illusion, for in almost all cases an expert derives more pleasure in applying his knowledge than in doing anything else. Corruption is different: here the local expert has little or nothing to offer in terms of graft, while his foreign counterpart has a lot.

The three major features that distinguish the North from the South underscore the need for unity in the latter. Yet countries of the South have more trading and other relations with the North than among themselves. They are also more interested in using the services of what Mazrui calls pure Northern experts than Southern ones who are resident in the North. The validity of this assertion is not conclusive. Almost all the Southern experts are induced or compelled to leave the South, and there are three types. The first type consists of those who are compelled for political reasons; a good example is Ugandans. The second type, who form the bulk, consists of those who migrate to the North for material and prestige reasons. They follow better pay, better terms of service, prestige, and nothing else. The third type is surely the tiniest: those who are sufficiently committed to research and knowledge as to move to the North in search of better working facilities rather than for material reward or prestige. This category find its home environment too hostile for academic pursuit: either the facilities are not there or the authorities do not recognize the importance of such rare experts. Thus it would seem futile to be interested in attracting Southern experts resident in the North.

Nonetheless, movement of experts within the South is a viable proposition. And according to Ali Mazrui, Egypt had at least until the recent economic and political changes in the Middle East, two million experts working in the Middle East and Africa. Also. there are Ghanaians working in the research complex of the University of Petroleum and Minerals in Dhahran in Saudi Arabia. Such exchanges should be encouraged and multiplied in Third World countries. Professor Mazrui also recommends trading among countries of the South by circumventing what he calls the bogey of foreign exchange. In this I am in complete agreement with him. Foreign exchange has been made something of a fetish to mystify the LDCs to the extent of suggesting that no trade and development could take place without it. Surely, foreign exchange is needed, but not to the level of making it a fetish. Therefore, there is ample room for barter in the development calculus of Southern countries. It is a very viable alternative: Nigeria has successfully tried it with Brazil; and countertrade is flourishing among some Third World countries and between them and some countries belonging to the Council for Mutual Economic Aid. Other countries are contemplating barter but are being lured away by IMF propagandists. There is no doubt that institutions like the IMF and IBRD would churn out literature containing veiled threats and mystifying arguments to destroy any initiative in barter trading. Hence there is only one solution: those interested in barter should ignore the critics and go ahead.

Lastly, unity as a foundation of organic and strategic solidarity is not sufficient. Some amount of autarky on the part of the Southern countries is necessary; it will enhance the chances of success in the struggle. In fact, I do not see hope for any development without the Third World countries drastically reducing the openness of their economies to the North. This is particularly relevant to the nations of Africa. Africa is very rich. Hence it should have a clear vision of what it wants to do and where it wants to go. Experience since independence has demonstrated that its development is incompatible with openness. Even if Africa could eventually develop while keeping its economy wide open to all the "garbage" from the industrialized countries, I am firmly convinced that it would take a very long time and that, by the time Africa "arrived," others would have plundered and exhausted its natural resources. So there are only two choices open to Africa: unity and some amount of autarky. For autarky, there is a lesson in a few Asian countries.

References

BOOKS

Abba, Alkasum, & Associates. *The Nigerian Economic Crisis: Causes and Solutions*. Zaria: Academic Staff Union of Nigerian Universities, 1985.

Amin, Samir. *Unequal Development: An Essay on the Social Formation of Peripheral Capitalism*. New York: Monthly Review Press, 1976.

Babu, A. Mohammed. *African Socialism or Socialist Africa*. Dar es Salaam and London: TPH and Zed Press, 1983.

Cline, W. R., & Associates. *World Inflation and the Developing Countries*. Washington, D.C.: Brookings Institution, 1981.

Dahrendorf, Ralf. *Life Chances: Approaches to Social and Political Theory*. Chicago: University of Chicago Press, 1981.

El Ghonemy, M. R., K. H. Parsons, R. P. Sinha, N. Uphoff, and P. Wignaraja. *Studies on Agrarian Reform and Rural Poverty*. Rome: Food and Agriculture Organization, 1984.

Gutkind, P. C. W., and Immanuel Wallerstein, eds. *The Political Economy of Contemporary Africa*. Beverly Hills, Calif.: Sage Publications, 1981.

Jalee, Pierre. *The Third World in World Economy*. New York: Monthly Review Press, 1971.

Kuznetz, Simon. *Towards a Theory of Economic Growth*. New York: W. W. Norton and Co., 1968.

Michaelson, K. L., ed. *And the Poor Get Children*. New York: Monthly Review Press, 1981.

Nabudere, D. Wadada. *The Political Economy of Imperialism*. 2d ed. Dar es Salaam and London: TPH and Zed Press, 1975.

Payer, Cheryl. *The Debt Trap: The IMF and the Third World*. New York: Monthly Review Press, 1974.

Poostchi, Iraj. *Rural Development and the Developing Countries: An Interdisciplinary Introductory Approach*. Guelph, Canada: 1986.

Robinson, Joan. *Aspects of Development and Underdevelopment*. London: Cambridge University Press, 1981.

Schumpeter, J. A. *The Theory of Economic Development*. New York: Oxford University Press, 1978.
Shonfield, Andrew (ed.), G. and V. Curzon, T. K. Warley, and George Ray. *International Economic Relations of the Western World, 1959-1971*. Vol. 1, *Politics and Trade*. London: Oxford University Press, 1976.
Thomas, C. Yolande. *Dependence and Transformation: The Economics of Transition to Socialism*. New York: Review Press, 1976.
Toffler, Alvin. *The Third Wave*. New York: Morrow, 1980.

REPORTS AND DOCUMENTS

Accelerated Development in Sub-Saharan Africa: An Agenda for Action. Washington, D.C.: World Bank, 1982.
CIRDAFRICA and African Economic Development. Arusha, Tanzania: CIRD-AFRICA, 1983.
Dimensions of Rural Crisis in Africa. Rome: FAO, 1985.
Famine in Africa: Situation, Cause, Prevention, Control. Rome: FAO, 1982.
FAO in Africa. Rome: FAO, 1981.
Forestry and Rural Development. Rome: FAO, 1981.
Forestry for Development. Rome: FAO, 1981.
Forestry for Rural Communities. Rome: FAO, 1984.
Guidelines for Designing Development Projects to Benefit the Rural Poor. Rome: FAO, 1984.
Harare Declaration on the Food Crisis of Africa. Rome: FAO, 1984.
Lagos Plan of Action for the Economic Development of Africa: 1980-2000. Addis Ababa: Organization of African Unity, 1981.
Proceedings of a Workshop on Energy, Forestry and Environment. Vol. 3. U.S. Agency for International Development, Addis Ababa, Bureau for Africa, 1982.
Proposals for Food and Agricultural Development 1986-1990. Addis Ababa: Economic Commission for Africa, 1985.
Public Expenditure on Agriculture in Developing Countries: 1978-82. Rome: FAO, 1984.
SADCC Agriculture Toward 2000. Rome: FAO, 1984.
Tipoteh, T. Dimensions of Rural Crisis in Africa. Rome: FAO, 1985.
Twenty-Five Years of Development Co-operation: Review. Paris: Organization for Economic Cooperation and Development, 1985.
WCARRD Follow-up Programme: How Rural Development Strategies Benefit the Rural Poor. Rome: FAO, 1984.
World Development Report. Washington, D.C.: World Bank, 1985.
World Economic Outlook. Washington, D.C.: International Monetary Fund, 1986.

PERIODICALS

Africa. No. 150. London: 1984.
AfricAsia. No. 29. Paris: May 1986.

African Business. London: July 1986.
African Farming and Food Processing. London: September-October 1985.
New African. London: November 1985.
Appropriate Technology. London: June, 1986.
Ceres. Rome: FAO.
Monthly Review. New York: Monthly Review Foundation.
International Business Week. New York: McGraw-Hill, August 12, 1985.
Newsletter No. 6. Rome: United Nations Administrative Committee on Coordination. Task Force, January–June 1986.
Rural Development 6. Rome: FAO, January–June 1986.
South. London: July and September, 1985.
World Water. Liverpool, May 1985.

SPEECHES

"Speech at U.N. Secretary General's Conference on African Food Problems." Geneva: March 11, 1985.
"Speech at the Institute of Social Studies, The Hague." The Hague: 13 March, 1985.
"Speech at the State Dinner President Veselin Djuranovic President of the Presidency of the Socialist Federal Republic of Yugoslavia." Belgrade: 14 March, 1985.
"Speech at the City of London Lunch." London: 18 March, 1985.
"Speech at the Royal Commonwealth Society Meeting." London: 20 March, 1985.

NEWSPAPERS

Daily News. Dar es Salaam.
Sunday News. Dar es Salaam.
National Concord. Lagos.

Index

About the Author

AHMAD ABUBAKAR is an economist with wide-ranging experience in African development. For the past fifteen years he has worked on development problems, both at the national and international level, in a variety of capacities and organizations. Presently, Mr. Abubakar serves as Acting Director of the Center for Integrated Rural Development for Africa (CIRDAFRICA) in Arusha, Tanzania.

Mr. Abubakar received his B.Sc. from the University of Ibadan and his M.A. from Vanderbilt University.